101 Things® To Do With A Bundt® Pan

101 Things® To Do With A Bundt® Pan

BY JENNY HARTIN

GIBBS SMITH
TO ENRICH AND INSPIRE HUMANKIND

First Edition
23 22 21 20   5 4 3

Text © 2019 Jenny Hartin

101 Things is a registered trademark of Gibbs Smith, Publisher
and Stephanie Ashcraft.
Bundt is a registered trademark of Northland Aluminum Products, Nordic Ware.

Chocolate Chip Scone Bread, page 23, courtesy of the Great Mrs. Larkin, Queen of Scones.
Esther's Sticky Buns, page 43, courtesy of Jean Johnson. Her mother Esther made these
buns frequently.
Sour Cream Pound Cake, page 107, and Lemon Blueberry Pound Cake, page 98,
courtesy of Lisa Ghenne, author of *The Cutting Edge of Ordinary* blog.

Published by
Gibbs Smith
P.O. Box 667
Layton, Utah 84041

1.800.835.4993 orders
www.gibbs-smith.com

Designed by Virginia Snow
Printed and bound in Korea

Gibbs Smith books are printed on either recycled, 100% post-consumer
waste, FSC-certified papers or on paper produced from sustainable PEFC-
certified forest/controlled wood source. Learn more at www.pefc.org.

Library of Congress Control Number: 2018968319
ISBN: 978-1-4236-5209-0

ACKNOWLEDGMENTS

Special thanks to my husband, Jim, and my sons Bryan and Andrew, who make cooking and baking a pleasure.

Thank you to my group of recipe testers: Judy A., Judy K., Rona, Faye, Renee, Robin C., Shellie, Dawn, Christine M., Allison C., Nancy, Lyla, and anyone else I may have forgotten! Thanks to my best friend Tina for her support and recipe suggestions.

And, to Robin Chesser who did an incredible job of editing, organizing, and making sense of my recipes.

Undying gratitude to Jane and Fiona of Eat Your Books for believing in me.

CONTENTS

Helpful Hints 9

Side Dishes

Potato Salad Bundt 64 • Macaroni and Cheese Bundt 65 • Rigatoni Bundt 66 • Pasta Salad with Crudite 67 • Sweet Potato Casserole 68 • Cheddar-Onion Bread Stuffing 69 • Macaroni and Cheese with Garlic Breadcrumbs 70 • Scalloped Potato Duo 71 • Bacon-Wrapped Loaded Mashed Potatoes 72 • Stuffed Spinach and Artichoke Bread 73 • Spicy Potato-Stuffed Naan Bundt 74 • Roasted Vegetables 76

Dinners

Turkey Meatloaf with Cranberry Sauce 78 • Cheese-Filled Italian Chicken Meatloaf 79 • Greek-Style Shepherd's Pie 80 • Stroganoff-Style Shepherd's Pie 81 • Roast Chicken Dinner 82 • Day-After-Thanksgiving in a Bundt 83 • Cacio e Pepe Spaghetti Bundt 84 • Chicken Enchilada Casserole 85 • Lemony Chicken Dinner 86 • Double Cornbread–Stuffed with Chili 87 • Patty Melt Casserole 88 • General Tso's Chicken 90 • Italian Chicken 91 • Zucchini Lasagna 92

Cakes

Brownie Chocolate Cake 94 • Celebration Cake 95 • Red Velvet Cake 96 • Italian Cassata Cake 97 • Lemon Blueberry Pound Cake 98 • Hummingbird Bundt 99 • Snickers-Filled Bundt 100 • Cream Cheese Pound Cake 101 • Funfetti Cake 102 • Citrus Overload Bundt Cake 103 • Zuccotto Bundt 104 • Harvey Wallbanger Cake 105 • Fourth of July Bundt 106 • Sour Cream Pound Cake 107 • Mascarpone-Oreo Filled Chocolate Cake 108 • Easy Ice Cream Cake 109 • Apple Dumpling Cake 110 • Strawberry Swirl Cream Cheese Pound Cake 111 • Pumpkin Pound Cake 112 • Berry-Filled Bundt Cake 113 • Holiday Fruit Cake 114

Desserts

Italian Flag Bundt 116 • Peach Crisp 117 • Chocolate Marshmallow Rice Crisp Ring 118 • Apple Cinnamon Dessert 119 • Jenny's Ice Cream Cake 120 • Peach Cobbler 121 • Strawberry Gelatin Mold 122 • Fruit Terrine 123 • Banana Pudding Dessert 124 • Cherry-Almond Gelatin Mold 125

HELPFUL HINTS

1. I recommend Nordic Ware Bundt Pans. They conduct heat well and are a high-quality product.

2. For purposes of the recipes in this book, a 10-inch or 12-cup Bundt pan is recommended and a tube-style Bundt pan with plain sides, when indicated, works more efficiently. The more elaborate pans will not work well here.

3. To prepare pans for cake-like recipes, I recommend an application of nonstick baking spray with flour, such as Baker's Joy, a light dusting of flour, tapping to release any excess flour, followed by another application of baking spray with flour before adding the batter.

4. For savory recipes, a liberal application of neutral-flavored nonstick cooking spray such as Pam works best.

5. Recipes call for all-purpose flour unless otherwise noted, eggs are always large, and I use Land O' Lakes butter for all my baking and cooking. Rhodes frozen bread is my preference when frozen bread is called for, and for cornbread mix (in lieu of making your own) I recommend Famous Dave's brand.

6. While some of these recipes call for packaged products, I always recommend using the highest quality ingredients for the best results. I only use Ghirardelli brand cake and brownie mixes as I find their quality unparalleled.

7. I recommend buying an instant-read digital thermometer to gauge your bread for doneness. Most breads are baked to an internal temperature of 190 degrees, and enriched breads to 200 degrees.

8. To check for doneness on cakes, use a Bundt cake tester or wooden skewer to insert into the cake. If it comes back clean, the cake is done. For cake-like brownies, remove from oven when they just begin to pull away from the sides of the pan, or a toothpick or skewer comes out clean. For fudgy brownies, bake within the time range stated in the recipe. For very moist brownies, remove from oven toward the minimum baking time.

9. The Nordic Ware anniversary pans in gold are workhorses and I display them on my kitchen wall for two reasons: space restrictions and they are decorative.

10. A thin flexible offset spatula is a great tool to help loosen the cooked contents from any troublesome Bundt pan.

11. Cooking dinner in a Bundt pan allows for even cooking as well as less splattering than when using a sheet pan.

BREADS

BROWN BREAD

1 cup	**flour**
2 cups	**whole-wheat flour**
1/4 cup plus 2 tablespoons	**sugar,** divided
2 teaspoons	**baking powder**
1 teaspoon	**baking soda**
1 teaspoon	**salt**
1/4 cup	**shortening**
1/4 cup	**buttermilk**
1 tablespoon	**water**
	butter, room temperature, optional
	marmalade or jam, of choice, optional

Preheat oven 375 degrees. Prepare a 6-cup Bundt pan with nonstick baking spray.

In a large bowl, add the flours, 1/4 cup sugar, baking powder, baking soda, and salt. Then cut the shortening into the dry ingredients with a pastry fork, pastry blender, or large fork. Add the buttermilk and mix until dough comes together; do not overmix.

Flour a work surface and knead dough about 10 times. Press lightly into a 7-inch circle, keeping an even thickness, and use a small round cutter to make a hole in the center of the dough. Place dough into the pan and mark with a small x in 4 evenly spaced places on the top of the dough. Bake for 40 minutes.

In a small saucepan, mix remaining sugar with 1 tablespoon of water and heat until sugar is dissolved. After bread has baked for 40 minutes, brush sugar mixture over the top of the loaf and bake for 5 more minutes. Remove from oven and allow to cool on a wire rack before inverting onto a platter. Serve slices with butter and marmalade, if desired. Makes 8–10 servings.

CRANBERRY AND ORANGE BREAD

2 cups	**flour**
1 1/2 teaspoons	**baking powder**
1/2 teaspoon	**baking soda**
1/2 teaspoon	**salt**
1 tablespoon	**orange zest**
1 1/2 cups	**fresh cranberries**
1/2 cup	**coarsely chopped pecans**
1/4 cup	**butter,** softened
1 cup	**sugar**
1	**egg,** room temperature
3/4 cup	**orange juice**

Preheat oven to 350 degrees. Prepare a 12-cup Bundt pan with nonstick baking spray.

In a medium bowl, whisk together the flour, baking powder, baking soda, and salt. Stir in orange zest, cranberries, and pecans. Set aside.

In a large bowl, cream together the butter, sugar, and egg until smooth. Mix in orange juice. Stir in flour mixture until just moistened. Pour batter into prepared pan.

Bake for 45–60 minutes, or until the bread springs back when lightly touched. Let rest in the pan for 10 minutes then turn out onto a wire rack to cool. Makes 10–12 servings.

LEMON POPPY SEED BREAD

2 cups	**flour**
1 1/2 teaspoons	**baking powder**
1/2 teaspoon	**baking soda**
1/2 teaspoon	**salt**
1 tablespoon	**lemon zest**
2 teaspoons	**poppy seeds**
1/4 cup	**butter,** softened
1 cup	**sugar**
1	**egg,** room temperature
1/2 cup	**lemon juice**
1/4 cup	**milk**

Glaze and Topping

1 cup	**powdered sugar**
1	**lemon,** zested and juiced
1/2 cup	**sliced almonds**

Preheat oven to 350 degrees. Prepare a 12-cup Bundt pan with nonstick baking spray.

In a medium bowl, whisk together flour, baking powder, baking soda, and salt. Stir in lemon zest and poppy seeds. Set aside.

In a large bowl, cream together butter, sugar, and egg until smooth. Mix in lemon juice. Stir in flour mixture alternating with milk until just moistened. Pour batter into prepared pan. Bake for 45–60 minutes, or until the bread springs back when lightly touched. Let rest in the pan for 10 minutes then turn out onto a wire rack to cool for 10 minutes.

Glaze and Topping In a small bowl, whisk together the powdered sugar and lemon zest and juice. Drizzle glaze over the bread and sprinkle almonds over top. Makes 10–12 servings.

GARLIC PARMESAN PULL-APART BREAD

I can (16.3 ounces)	**refrigerated biscuits** (not the flaky kind)
4 tablespoons	**butter,** melted
2 cloves	**garlic,** minced
1/2 cup	**freshly grated Parmesan cheese,** plus extra
	marinara sauce, warmed

Preheat oven to 350 degrees. Prepare a 12-cup Bundt pan with nonstick baking spray.

Cut the biscuits into quarters and place in a medium bowl. Add the butter, garlic, and Parmesan; toss to coat. Layer coated biscuit pieces into prepared pan and bake for 20–25 minutes.

Remove from oven and let cool for 10 minutes before inverting onto a serving platter. Sprinkle more Parmesan cheese over top of bread, if desired. Serve with marinara sauce on the side for dipping. Makes 10–12 servings.

EVERYTHING BAGEL LOAF

1 can (16.3 ounces)	**refrigerated biscuits** (not the flaky kind)
4 tablespoons	**butter,** melted
1 teaspoon	**granulated onion**
1 teaspoon	**granulated garlic**
1 teaspoon	**sesame seeds**
1 teaspoon	**poppy seeds**
$^1/_2$ teaspoon	**sea salt**
	cream cheese spread, optional

Preheat oven to 350 degrees. Prepare a 12-cup Bundt pan with nonstick baking spray.

Cut the biscuits into quarters and place in a medium bowl. Add the butter, onion, garlic, sesame and poppy seeds, and salt; toss to coat. Layer coated pieces into prepared pan and bake for 20–25 minutes.

Remove from oven, and let cool for 10 minutes before inverting onto a serving platter. Serve with cream cheese, if desired. Makes 10–12 servings.

BANANA BREAD WITH PEANUT BUTTER GLAZE

8 tablespoons	**butter,** softened
6	**overripe bananas,** mashed
1 1/3 cups	**sugar**
2 2/3 cups	**flour**
4	**eggs,** room temperature
1 1/2 teaspoons	**salt**
1 teaspoon	**baking soda**
1/2 teaspoon	**baking powder**
1/4 cup	**peanut butter**
1 1/4 cups	**powdered sugar**
3 teaspoons plus more	**milk**
	crushed peanuts, optional

Preheat oven to 350 degrees. Prepare a 12-cup Bundt pan with nonstick baking spray.

In a large bowl, thoroughly combine together the butter, bananas, sugar, flour, eggs, salt, baking soda, and baking powder. Spread batter evenly into the prepared pan and bake for 60 minutes, checking for doneness after 45 minutes. After the tester comes out clean, allow bread to cool on rack for 10 minutes before inverting onto a serving platter; let cool for 15 more minutes.

In a medium bowl, mix together the peanut butter, powdered sugar, and 3 teaspoons milk until smooth. If a thinner, pourable consistency is preferred, add 3 more teaspoons milk. Spread or drizzle glaze over top of bread. Sprinkle with peanuts, if desired. Makes 10–12 servings.

SALLY LUNN BREAD

I cup	**milk**
5 tablespoons	**vegetable shortening**
1/3 cup	**sugar**
4 cups	**flour,** divided
2 teaspoons	**salt**
2 envelopes (1/4 ounce each)	**active dry yeast**
3	**eggs,** beaten

In a medium saucepan, heat milk, shortening, and sugar until warm and shortening has melted; remove from heat and cool to lukewarm.

In a large mixer bowl, whisk together 1 1/2 cups flour, salt, and yeast. Add the milk mixture to the flour mixture and combine. Then beat on medium speed for 2 minutes. Gradually add 1/2 cup flour and eggs then beat on high speed for 2 minutes. Mix in remaining flour (batter will be thick).

Cover bowl and place in a warm area. Let rise until double in size, approximately 60 minutes. Punch the dough down and beat on low speed for a few seconds.

Preheat oven to 350 degrees. Prepare a 12-cup Bundt or tube pan with nonstick baking spray.

Place dough in pan, cover, and let rise until dough increases by 1/3 the size. Bake for 40 minutes, or until crust is a deep golden brown.

Remove from oven and loosen sides and center with a knife and turn onto a plate just like a cake. Cut into slices and serve warm. Makes 10–12 servings.

BUNDT PANETTONE

2 1/4 cups	**flour,** divided
1/3 cup	**sugar**
2 1/2 teaspoons	**active dry yeast**
1/2 teaspoon	**salt**
1/2 cup	**milk,** warmed (100 degrees)
1/4 cup	**butter,** softened
3	**eggs,** room temperature
1/2 teaspoon	**vanilla**
2/3 cup	**dried cranberries, cherries, or raisins**
1/2 cup	**candied fruit or ginger,** optional
	powdered sugar, optional

Rum Syrup

1/2 cup	**sugar**
1/3 cup	**rum**

Prepare a 12-cup Bundt pan with butter or nonstick baking spray.

In a large bowl, stir together 3/4 cup flour, sugar, yeast, and salt. Add the milk and butter and beat for 2 minutes at medium speed until smooth. Add the eggs, 1 at a time, beating well after each addition. Stir in vanilla. Add 1/2 cup flour and beat for 2 more minutes at medium-high speed. Stir in remaining flour to create a thick batter; cover bowl and let rest for 10 minutes. Stir in cranberries and candied fruit, if using. Pour into the pan, cover, and let rise in a warm place until double in size, about 2 hours.

Preheat oven to 350 degrees. Bake bread for 30–35 minutes, or until golden and top springs back when lightly touched. Remove panettone from oven and pierce the surface multiple times with a skewer.

To prepare Rum Syrup, combine the sugar and rum in a small saucepan over medium heat. Cook, stirring, until sugar dissolves. Bring to a boil and then remove from heat.

Pour hot syrup over bread and allow to soak in. Let stand for 15 minutes then remove bread from pan and cool completely on a wire rack. Dust with powdered sugar before serving. Makes 10–12 servings.

DOUBLE CORNBREAD

1 cup	**self-rising white cornmeal mix**
1/2 cup	**self-rising flour,** sifted
1/4 cup	**corn muffin mix**
2 tablespoons	**sugar**
2	**eggs,** beaten
1 can (14.75 ounces)	**cream-style corn**
1 cup	**buttermilk**
	butter, optional
	honey or maple syrup, optional

Preheat oven to 400 degrees. Prepare a 12-cup Bundt pan with nonstick baking spray.

In medium bowl, combine cornmeal mix, flour, muffin mix, sugar, eggs, corn, and buttermilk. Stir until well-combined and pourable. Small lumps are okay. Set aside.

Place the empty pan into the hot oven for 5 minutes. Remove carefully from oven and spread batter into the hot pan.

Reduce oven temperature to 350 degrees. Bake for 25–30 minutes, check for doneness using a toothpick or skewer. Cool on rack for 10 minutes before inverting onto serving plate. Serve with butter, honey, or maple syrup, if desired. Makes 8 servings.

GOLDEN MILK BUNDT BREAD

2 tablespoons	**active dry yeast**
1 tablespoon	**warm water**
1 tablespoon plus 1 teaspoon	**sugar,** divided
3 cups	**flour**
1 teaspoon	**salt**
7 tablespoons	**powdered milk**
³/₄ cup	**warm milk**
¹/₄ cup	**heavy cream**
2 tablespoons	**canola oil,** divided
1 ¹/₂ tablespoons	**milk**
3 tablespoons	**salted butter,** melted
1 teaspoon	**honey**
¹/₂ teaspoon	**ground turmeric**
dash of	**ground cinnamon**
dash of	**ground ginger**

Prepare a 12-cup Bundt pan with nonstick baking spray. In a small bowl, add the yeast, warm water, and 1 teaspoon sugar. Let rest for 5 minutes.

In large bowl, mix together flour, salt, 1 tablespoon sugar, and powdered milk. Make a well in the center of the dry ingredients. Add the warm milk, cream, 1 tablespoon oil, and yeast mixture; stir. Place the dough onto a lightly floured surface and knead for at least 5 minutes. Add the remaining oil and knead for several minutes until the dough is soft and smooth. Place dough back in bowl, cover with a clean kitchen towel, and set in a warm place for about 1 hour or until double in size. Punch down dough and knead for about 1 minute. Divide dough into 8 balls and place in the pan. Cover with a clean kitchen towel. Place in a warm area to rise again until double in size.

Preheat oven to 350 degrees. In a small bowl, mix together the 1 ¹/₂ tablespoons milk, butter, honey, and spices; brush over the dough. Cover the pan with aluminum foil and bake for 30 minutes; remove foil after 10 minutes. Continue baking, uncovered, for the remaining 20 minutes. Check for doneness and remove from oven. Brush with additional butter. Makes 10–12 servings.

CARROT CAKE BREAD

I box (15.25 ounces)	**carrot cake mix**
1/2 cup	**chopped walnuts**
I can (15 ounces)	**pineapple chunks,** drained
4	**eggs,** room temperature
1/2 cup	**sugar**
1 1/2 cups	**milk**
I tablespoon	**vanilla**
I teaspoon	**ground cinnamon**
1/2 teaspoon	**ground ginger, or 1/4 teaspoon grated fresh ginger**
I recipe	**Cream Cheese Frosting** (page 96), optional

Preheat oven to 350 degrees. Prepare a 9 x 13-inch pan and a 12-cup Bundt pan with nonstick baking spray.

Prepare cake mix according to the package directions and bake in the 9 x 13-inch pan for 30 minutes (do not overbake). Allow to cool 10 minutes in the pan. Remove and cool completely. Cut cake into 1-inch cubes. Layer cake cubes, walnuts, and pineapple in prepared Bundt pan.

In a medium bowl, beat together the eggs, sugar, milk, vanilla, cinnamon, and ginger until well-blended; pour evenly over contents of Bundt pan. Bake 45 minutes, or until edges start to pull away from sides. Cool 10 minutes. Loosen edges and invert onto a serving platter. Drizzle glaze over top, or serve on the side for dipping, if desired. Makes 12 servings.

CHOCOLATE CHIP SCONE BREAD

2 tablespoons	**butter,** softened
3 tablespoons plus extra	**sugar,** divided
pinch of	**ground cinnamon**
2$^1/_2$ cups plus I teaspoon	**flour,** divided
2 teaspoons	**baking powder**
$^3/_4$ teaspoon	**salt**
6 tablespoons	**unsalted butter,** chilled, diced
I cup plus extra	**heavy cream**
I	**egg**
2 teaspoons	**vanilla,** divided
I cup	**semisweet chocolate chips**
$^1/_2$ cup	**sifted powdered sugar**
3–4 tablespoons	**milk**

Preheat oven to 375 degrees. Prepare a 12-cup Bundt pan with 2 tablespoons butter. In a small bowl, mix together I tablespoon sugar and cinnamon; sprinkle in the bottom of the pan.

In a food processor, pulse together 2$^1/_2$ cups flour, remaining sugar, baking powder, and salt. Add the chilled butter and pulse about 8 times; place the mixture into a bowl.

In a large measuring cup, mix together the cream, egg, and I$^1/_2$ teaspoons vanilla. Pour into the flour mixture. In a small bowl, toss the chocolate chips with I teaspoon flour, to coat. Add the chocolate and the cream mixture to the flour mixture. Fold the ingredients together to form a dough; do not overmix. Transfer dough onto a floured work surface and pat into a 6 x 14-inch rectangle. Cut the rectangle into 14 equal squares. Brush with cream and sprinkle with sugar. Layer the scones in the pan beside each other.

Bake for about 50 minutes, checking after 30–40 minutes. If browning too quickly, cover with aluminum foil. Test for doneness with a cake tester. Remove from oven and let cool for 15 minutes; carefully invert scones onto a serving platter. Mix powdered sugar, remaining vanilla, and milk together until smooth; drizzle over scones. Makes 8–10 servings.

MONKEY
BREADS

ORIGINAL MONKEY BREAD

¹/₂ cup	**sugar**
1 teaspoon	**ground cinnamon**
2 cans (16.3 ounces each)	**large refrigerated biscuits**
¹/₂ cup	**chopped walnuts,** optional
1 cup	**firmly packed brown sugar**
³/₄ cup	**butter,** melted

Preheat oven to 350 degrees. Prepare a 12-cup Bundt pan with nonstick baking spray.

In a large bowl, mix the sugar and cinnamon.

Separate the dough into 16 biscuits; cut each into quarters. Toss in the bowl to coat with sugar mixture. Arrange the biscuit pieces evenly in prepared pan, sprinkling walnuts throughout, if using.

In small bowl, mix the brown sugar and butter; pour over biscuit pieces. Bake for 30–35 minutes, until golden brown and no longer doughy in center. Cool in pan for 10 minutes. Turn upside down onto a serving plate; pull apart to serve. Serve warm. Makes 8 servings.

LEMON-WHITE CHOCOLATE MONKEY BREAD

1 1/2 cups	**sugar,** divided
3 teaspoons	**lemon zest,** divided
2 cans (16.3 ounces each)	**large refrigerated biscuits**
1/2 cup	**sliced almonds,** optional
1/2–1 cup	**chopped good-quality white chocolate**
1/4 cup	**fresh lemon juice**
3/4 cup	**butter,** melted

Preheat oven to 350 degrees. Prepare a 12-cup Bundt pan with nonstick baking spray.

In a large bowl, mix 1/2 cup of sugar and 1 teaspoon lemon zest.

Separate the dough into 16 biscuits; cut each into quarters. Toss in the bowl to coat with sugar mixture. Arrange the biscuit pieces evenly in prepared pan, sprinkling almonds, white chocolate, and remaining lemon zest throughout.

In small bowl, mix the remaining sugar, lemon juice, and butter; pour over biscuit pieces.

Bake for 30–35 minutes, until golden brown and no longer doughy in center. Cool in pan for 10 minutes. Turn upside down onto a serving plate; pull apart to serve. Serve warm. Makes 8 servings.

STRAWBERRY SHORTCAKE MONKEY BREAD

1 1/2 cups	**sugar,** divided
1 teaspoon	**fresh thyme,** finely minced
2 cans (16.3 ounces each)	**large refrigerated biscuits**
2 cups	**chopped fresh strawberries**
1/2 cup	**strawberry jam**
3/4 cup	**butter,** melted
1/2 cup	**heavy cream**
	whipped cream, optional

Preheat oven to 350 degrees. Prepare a 12-cup Bundt pan with nonstick baking spray.

In a large bowl, mix 1/2 cup of sugar and thyme.

Separate the dough into 16 biscuits; cut each into quarters. Toss in the bowl to coat with sugar mixture. Arrange the biscuit pieces evenly in prepared pan, distributing the strawberries and dolloping the jam throughout.

In small bowl, mix remaining sugar, butter, and cream; pour over biscuit pieces.

Bake for 30–35 minutes, until golden brown and no longer doughy in center. Cool in pan for 10 minutes. Turn upside down onto a serving plate; pull apart to serve. Serve warm with fresh whipped cream, if desired. Makes 8 servings.

S'MORES MONKEY BREAD

1/2 cup	**sugar**
1/2 cup	**graham cracker crumbs**
2 cans (16.3 ounces each)	**large refrigerated biscuits**
1 cup	**good-quality semisweet chocolate chips**
1 cup	**mini marshmallows**
1 cup	**firmly packed brown sugar**
3/4 cup	**butter,** melted

Preheat oven to 350 degrees. Prepare a 12-cup Bundt pan with nonstick baking spray.

In a large bowl, mix the sugar and graham cracker crumbs.

Separate the dough into 16 biscuits; cut each into quarters. Toss in the bowl to coat with sugar mixture. Arrange the biscuit pieces evenly in prepared pan, sprinkling chocolate and marshmallows throughout.

In small bowl, mix the brown sugar and butter; pour over biscuit pieces.

Bake for 30–35 minutes, until golden brown and no longer doughy in center. Cool in pan for 10 minutes. Turn upside down onto a serving plate; pull apart to serve. Serve warm. Makes 8 servings.

HAWAIIAN MONKEY BREAD

1 1/4 cups	**sugar,** divided
3 tablespoons	**finely chopped macadamia nuts**
1/3 cup	**butter,** melted
1 can (8 ounces)	**crushed pineapple,** drained, juice reserved
1/2 cup	**shredded coconut**
2 cans (16.3 ounces each)	**large refrigerated biscuits**
3 ounces	**cream cheese,** softened

Preheat oven to 350 degrees. Prepare a 12-cup Bundt pan with nonstick baking spray.

In a pie plate, mix 1 cup of sugar and the nuts. Pour the butter into another pie plate or a bowl. In large bowl, combine the pineapple and coconut.

Separate the dough into 16 biscuits. Cut each biscuit in half. Dip both sides of biscuit halves into the butter then roll in sugar mixture to coat all sides. Mix biscuit pieces with pineapple and coconut. Arrange pieces in prepared pan.

Bake for 25–35 minutes, until light golden brown. Cool for 5 minutes before inverting onto a serving plate; cool for an additional 5 minutes.

While bread is cooling, beat the cream cheese and remaining sugar with electric mixer on medium speed for 30–45 seconds, until smooth. Beat in 1 tablespoon of the reserved pineapple juice then add 1 teaspoon at a time until thin enough to drizzle. Drizzle over hot monkey bread. Serve warm. Makes 8–10 servings.

SAVORY LEMON, THYME, AND GRUYERE MONKEY BREAD

6 tablespoons	**butter,** melted
$^1/_2$ teaspoon	**garlic salt**
1 teaspoon	**lemon zest**
$^1/_2$ teaspoon	**minced fresh thyme**
2 cans (16.3 ounces each)	**large refrigerated biscuits**
$^1/_2$ cup	**grated Gruyere cheese**
	grated Parmesan cheese, optional
	melted butter, optional

Preheat oven to 350 degrees. Prepare a 12-cup Bundt pan with nonstick baking spray.

In a large bowl, mix the butter, garlic salt, lemon zest, and thyme.

Separate dough into 16 biscuits; cut each into quarters. Toss in the bowl to coat with butter mixture. Arrange the biscuit pieces evenly in pan, sprinkling the Gruyere throughout.

Bake for 30–35 minutes, until golden brown and no longer doughy in center. Cool in pan for 10 minutes. Turn upside down onto a serving plate; pull apart to serve. Serve warm. Sprinkle with Parmesan or drizzle with butter, if desired. Makes 8 servings.

BREAD
PUDDINGS

CHOCOLATE PEANUT BUTTER BREAD PUDDING

12 cups	**cubed stale croissants** (about 9–10 large croissants)
2 cups	**semisweet chocolate chunks or chips**
6	**eggs**
2 cups	**milk**
1 cup	**sugar**
1 cup	**creamy or crunchy peanut butter**
1 teaspoon	**vanilla**
	hot fudge sauce, optional

Prepare a 12-cup Bundt pan with nonstick baking spray. Distribute the croissants evenly in the pan. Sprinkle with chocolate.

In a large bowl, whisk the eggs until lightly beaten. Add the milk, sugar, peanut butter, and vanilla; whisk until combined. Pour the mixture over the croissants. If necessary, press the croissants down into the egg mixture to coat. Refrigerate for at least 1 hour or overnight.

Remove the chilled bread pudding from the refrigerator and let set at room temperature for about 30 minutes.

Preheat oven to 350 degrees.

Bake for 60–70 minutes, until a skewer inserted into the center of the pudding comes out clean. Allow to cool for 15 minutes before carefully inverting onto a serving platter. Serve with hot fudge sauce, if desired. Makes 12 servings.

WHITE CHOCOLATE, ALMOND, AND CRANBERRY BREAD PUDDING

12 cups	**cubed stale croissants** (about 9–10 large croissants)
1 1/2 cups	**chunks good-quality white chocolate**
6	**eggs**
2 cups	**milk**
1/2 cup	**sugar**
1 teaspoon	**vanilla**
1 cup	**fresh cranberries**
1 cup	**sliced almonds**
	creme anglaise, optional

Prepare a 12-cup Bundt pan with nonstick baking spray. Distribute the croissants evenly in the pan. Sprinkle with white chocolate.

In a large bowl, whisk the eggs until lightly beaten. Add the milk, sugar, and vanilla; whisk until combined. Toss in the cranberries and almonds. Pour the mixture over the croissants. If necessary, press the croissants down into the egg mixture to coat. Refrigerate for at least 1 hour or overnight.

Remove the chilled bread pudding from the refrigerator and let set at room temperature for about 30 minutes.

Preheat oven to 350 degrees.

Bake the bread pudding for 60–70 minutes, or until a skewer inserted into the center of the pudding comes out clean. Allow to cool for 15 minutes before carefully inverting onto a serving platter. Serve with bowl of creme anglaise for drizzling, if desired. Makes 12 servings.

MAPLE-PECAN BREAD PUDDING

12 cups	**cubed stale sourdough bread**
6	**eggs**
1/2 cup	**firmly packed brown sugar**
2 cups	**milk**
1/4 cup	**maple syrup**
1 1/2 cups	**chopped pecans**
	maple syrup, warmed, optional
	butter, room temperature, optional

Preheat oven to 350 degrees. Prepare a 12-cup Bundt pan with nonstick baking spray.

Place the bread in a large bowl.

In another large bowl, whisk together the eggs and brown sugar. Add the milk and maple syrup; whisk until combined. Whisk in the pecans. Pour mixture over the bread and stir to combine. Pour the mixture into the prepared pan.

Bake for 1 hour, or until a skewer inserted into the center of the pudding comes out clean. Allow to cool for 15 minutes before carefully inverting onto a serving platter. Serve with maple syrup and butter, if desired. Makes 12 servings.

PINEAPPLE, CHEDDAR, AND HAM BREAD PUDDING

12 cups	**cubed stale bread,** of choice
6	**eggs**
2 cups	**milk**
I can (14 ounces)	**pineapple chunks,** drained
I cup	**grated cheddar cheese**
I cup	**diced cooked ham**

Preheat oven to 350 degrees. Prepare a 12-cup Bundt pan with nonstick baking spray.

Place the bread in a large bowl.

In another large bowl, whisk the eggs until lightly beaten. Add the milk and whisk until combined. Stir in the pineapple, cheese, and ham. Pour the mixture over the bread and stir to combine. Pour the mixture into the prepared pan.

Bake for I hour, or until a skewer inserted into the center of the pudding comes out clean. Allow to cool for 15 minutes before carefully inverting onto a serving platter. Makes 12 servings.

This is a wonderful side dish for Easter brunch.

APPLE PIE BREAD PUDDING

12 cups	**cubed stale croissants** (about 9–10 large croissants)
6	**eggs**
1/2 cup	**firmly packed brown sugar**
2 cups	**milk**
1 teaspoon	**apple pie spice**
1 1/2 cups	**chopped walnuts**
1 1/2 cups	**diced apples**
	caramel sauce, warmed, optional
	vanilla ice cream, optional

Preheat oven to 350 degrees. Prepare a 12-cup Bundt pan with nonstick baking spray.

Place the croissants in a large bowl.

In another large bowl, whisk together the eggs and brown sugar. Whisk in the milk and apple pie spice until combined. Stir in the walnuts and apples. Pour over the croissants and stir to combine.

Transfer the mixture to the prepared pan and bake for 1 hour, or until a skewer inserted into the center of the pudding comes out clean. Allow to cool for 15 minutes before carefully inverting onto a serving platter. Serve with caramel sauce and vanilla ice cream, if desired. Makes 12 servings.

CROISSANT CUSTARD BREAD PUDDING

6	**eggs**
3/4–1 cup	**sugar**
1 teaspoon	**vanilla**
3 cups	**milk**
6	**large day-old croissants**

Preheat oven to 300 degrees. Prepare a 12-cup Bundt pan with nonstick baking spray.

In a medium bowl, lightly beat the eggs then whisk in the sugar until dissolved. Add the vanilla and milk; whisk until combined.

Tear croissants into large pieces and place into a large bowl. Pour custard over croissants and allow to soak for up 30 minutes.

Transfer mixture to pan and bake for 1 hour, until pudding is firmly set and the top is browned. Turn the oven off and let the pudding cool inside for 20 minutes. Remove from oven, carefully loosen the pudding with a knife, and invert onto a serving platter. Makes 10 servings.

VARIATION: Before serving, sprinkle coarse sugar over the top of the pudding and use a kitchen torch to caramelize until bubbly.

CHEESY MEATY BREAD PUDDING

5 tablespoons	**unsalted butter,** divided
3	**onions,** halved and thinly sliced
8 stalks	**celery,** thinly sliced
12 slices	**sourdough bread,** lightly toasted
	salt and pepper, to taste
2 tablespoons	**fresh thyme**
2 tablespoons	**minced fresh Italian parsley**
10 ounces	**pepperoni,** cut into small cubes
1 pound	**ground pork sausage**
1 pound	**mozzarella cheese,** cut into $^1/_2$-inch cubes
1 cup	**chicken stock,** heated

Preheat oven to 375 degrees. Prepare a 12-cup Bundt pan with nonstick baking spray.

In a large skillet over medium heat, melt 2 tablespoons butter. Add onions and celery and saute for 5 minutes. Transfer to a bowl; set aside.

Cut the toast into 1-inch squares and transfer to a large bowl. Melt 2 tablespoons butter and drizzle over the bread. Add salt and pepper, and then add the thyme and parsley. Toss everything together and set aside.

Heat remaining butter in a large skillet over high heat. Add the pepperoni and cook, stirring, for 2–3 minutes. Drain on paper towels. Add the sausage to the skillet and cook, stirring and breaking into small pieces, until browned, about 10 minutes; drain excess grease.

Add the celery mixture, pepperoni, sausage, and mozzarella to the bread. Stir to combine, add the stock to moisten all the ingredients, and stir again.

Pour the mixture into the prepared pan and cover with aluminum foil. Bake for 30 minutes then remove the foil and continue baking until golden brown, about 25 more minutes. Makes 10–12 servings.

BREAKFASTS

CINNAMON PECAN BREAKFAST

Pecan Streusel

1/2 cup	**firmly packed brown sugar**
1/2 cup	**flour**
1 teaspoon	**ground cinnamon**
1/4 cup	**butter**
3/4 cup	**chopped pecans**

Pound Cake Batter

1 cup	**butter,** softened
2 1/2 cups	**sugar**
6	**eggs,** room temperature
3 cups	**flour**
1/4 teaspoon	**baking soda**
1 container (8 ounces)	**sour cream**
2 teaspoons	**vanilla**
1 cup	**finely chopped pecans,** toasted
1/4 cup	**firmly packed brown sugar**
1 1/2 teaspoons	**ground cinnamon**

Preheat oven to 325 degrees. Prepare a 12-cup Bundt pan with nonstick baking spray. Prepare the streusel by combining brown sugar, flour, and cinnamon in a small bowl. Cut in butter with a pastry blender until mixture resembles small peas. Stir in pecans and set aside.

For the cake batter, place the butter in a large mixing bowl and beat at medium speed until creamy. Gradually add the sugar, beating until light and fluffy. Add eggs, 1 at a time, beating after each addition. Stir together flour and baking soda; add to butter mixture alternating with sour cream. Beat at low speed just until blended. Stir in vanilla.

Pour half of the batter into the pan. In a small bowl, stir together the pecans, brown sugar, and cinnamon; sprinkle over batter. Spoon remaining batter over pecan mixture; sprinkle with the streusel. Bake for 60–75 minutes, or until a skewer inserted into the center comes out clean. Cool in pan on a wire rack 10–15 minutes; remove from pan to wire rack, and cool completely. Makes 8–10 servings.

ESTHER'S STICKY BUNS

3/4 cup	**sugar**
pinch of	**salt**
1 1/2 teaspoons	**ground cinnamon**
1 loaf (1 pound)	**frozen white bread dough,**
	thawed overnight
1/2 cup	**butter,** melted
3/4 cup	**heavy cream**

Prepare a 6-cup Bundt pan with nonstick baking spray.

Mix together the sugar, salt, and cinnamon in a shallow bowl.

Cut the dough into 40–50 small pieces. With lightly oiled or buttered hands, roll each piece of dough into a ball and then into the melted butter; roll in the sugar mixture and stack the balls evenly, so that they are touching in the pan. Drizzle any remaining butter over the top and sprinkle with any of the remaining sugar mixture. Pour the cream over and around the dough balls and then place the pan on the stovetop while preheating the oven.

Preheat oven to 400 degrees.

Bake for about 30 minutes, or until the cream is bubbling and the buns are nicely browned and firm to the touch. Remove from the oven and wait a couple of minutes for the bubbling to subside. Then, take a large platter, place it upside down over the hot pan and invert the hot rolls onto the platter. Makes 8 servings.

BACON-WRAPPED BREAKFAST BUNDT

1 pound	**bacon**
2 cups	**frozen potato tots**
12	**eggs,** whisked
6 slices	**stale sourdough bread,** diced
2 cups	**grated cheese,** of choice
$^1/_4$ cup	**whole milk**
$^1/_2$	**onion,** diced and sauteed in butter
	salt and pepper, to taste

Preheat oven to 400 degrees. Prepare a 12-cup Bundt pan with nonstick cooking spray.

Cut the strips of bacon in half crosswise and line the bottom of the pan with the bacon.

In a large bowl, mix together the tots, eggs, bread, cheese, milk, onion, and salt and pepper. Spoon the mixture carefully over the bacon strips so they don't move. Bake for 45 minutes.

Remove from oven and rest for 10 minutes before inverting onto a platter. Cut into slices to serve. Makes 8–10 servings.

VEGGIE BREAKFAST CASSEROLE

2 cups	**frozen potato tots**
12	**eggs,** whisked
I cup	**broccoli florets,** diced
2 cups	**grated cheese,** of choice
$^1/_4$ cup	**whole milk**
$^1/_2$ cup	**diced onion,** sauteed in butter
	salt and pepper, to taste
$^1/_2$	**red bell pepper,** diced, optional
pinch of	**dried red pepper flakes,** optional

Preheat oven to 400 degrees. Prepare a 12-cup Bundt pan with nonstick cooking spray.

In a large bowl, mix together the tots, eggs, broccoli, cheese, milk, onion, salt and pepper, and bell pepper and pepper flakes, if using. Spoon mixture into the pan. Bake for 45 minutes.

Remove from oven and rest for 10 minutes before inverting onto a platter. Cut into slices to serve. Makes 8–10 servings.

CINNAMON ROLLS IN A BUNDT

2 cans (12.4 ounces)	**Pillsbury Cinnamon Rolls**
3 tablespoons	**butter**
1/2 cup	**firmly packed brown sugar**
1 cup	**chopped pecans**

Preheat oven to 350 degrees. Prepare a 12-cup Bundt pan with nonstick cooking spray.

Line the pan with the cinnamon rolls; reserving the frosting. Bake for 20 minutes.

In a small saucepan, melt the butter and brown sugar together; stir in the pecans. Cook, stirring, until sugar is completely dissolved and incorporated with the butter.

Remove rolls from oven and rest for 5 minutes before inverting onto a serving platter. Pour warm pecan mixture over the top of the rolls. Drizzle with frosting if desired, or serve the frosting in a small bowl on the side. Makes 8–10 servings.

POTATO AND EGG BREAKFAST

2 cups	**frozen potato tots**
12	**eggs,** whisked
I can (16.3 ounce)	**Pillsbury Grands biscuits,** diced
2 cups	**grated cheese,** of choice
$^1/_4$ cup	**whole milk**
	salt and pepper, to taste
$^1/_2$ cup	**diced onion,** sauteed in butter, optional
I cup	**diced ham,** optional

Preheat oven to 400 degrees. Prepare a 12-cup Bundt pan with nonstick cooking spray.

In a large bowl, combine the tots, eggs, biscuit pieces, cheese, milk, salt and pepper, onion, if using, and ham, if using. Place in the prepared pan. Bake for 45 minutes.

Remove from oven and rest for 10 minutes before inverting onto a platter. Cut into slices to serve. Makes 8–10 servings.

JELLY DOUGHNUT BUNDT

3 1/2 cups	**flour**
1 3/4 cups	**sugar,** divided
1 1/2 teaspoons	**baking powder**
1/2 teaspoon	**baking soda**
1/2 teaspoon	**salt**
1 2/3 cups	**buttermilk**
1 cup	**vegetable oil**
3	**eggs,** room temperature, beaten
2 teaspoons	**vanilla**
1/2 cup	**good quality strawberry jam,** or flavor of choice
3 tablespoons	**melted butter**
1 teaspoon	**ground cinnamon**

Preheat oven to 350 degrees. Prepare a 12-cup Bundt pan with nonstick baking spray.

In a large mixing bowl, combine the flour, 1 1/2 cups sugar, baking powder, baking soda, and salt. In a separate bowl, mix together the buttermilk, oil, eggs, and vanilla. Add the wet ingredients to the dry ingredients and mix until just combined.

Pour the batter into the pan and drop small spoonfuls of jam into and around the center of the batter. Gently pull a long skewer through the jam to swirl. Bake for 45 minutes, or until a skewer inserted near the center comes out clean.

Cool in pan on a wire rack for 15 minutes. Invert the cake onto a plate. Brush with the melted butter. Combine remaining sugar and cinnamon together, and sprinkle very generously over top. Makes 10–12 servings.

CHOCOLATE HAZELNUT-FILLED BREAKFAST BUNDT

I cup	**chocolate hazelnut spread**
1/2 cup	**cream cheese,** softened
1/2 cup	**sugar**
1/2 cup	**firmly packed brown sugar**
I 1/2 teaspoons	**ground cinnamon**
dash of	**freshly grated nutmeg**
I loaf (I pound)	**frozen white bread dough,** thawed overnight
1/2 cup	**butter,** melted
I cup	**chopped toasted hazelnuts**
3/4 cup	**heavy cream**
	powdered sugar, optional

Preheat oven to 350 degrees. Prepare a 12-cup Bundt pan with nonstick baking spray.

Place the hazelnut spread and cream cheese in a small microwave-safe bowl and microwave for 20 seconds to soften. Stir to combine. In a small bowl, mix together the sugars, cinnamon, and nutmeg.

Evenly divide the dough into 30 pieces. Flatten each piece of dough into a disk and spoon about 1 1/2 teaspoons of the chocolate spread into the center. Pinch the dough around the edges to seal and form a ball. Dip balls in the butter and then roll in sugar mixture. Sprinkle some hazelnuts into the bottom of the pan and layer in the coated balls, sprinkling hazelnuts between layers. Cover with a clean kitchen towel and allow to rise for at least 30 minutes until almost double in size.

Pour the cream over the bread and place in the oven. Bake for 20 minutes then reduce temperature to 325 degrees; continue to bake for 10 additional minutes until bread is done. Cool in pan on a rack for 10 minutes before inverting onto a serving platter. Dust with powdered sugar, if desired; serve warm. Makes 8–10 servings.

EGGY BREAKFAST BAKE

2 cups	**chopped fresh spinach**
I teaspoon	**olive oil**
I teaspoon	**salt,** divided, plus extra, to taste
$^3/_4$ teaspoon	**pepper,** divided, plus extra, to taste
$^1/_4$ teaspoon	**garlic powder**
2 cups	**frozen shredded hash browns**
8 cups ($^3/_4$-inch cubes)	**sourdough bread**
$^1/_4$ cup	**chopped green onions**
2 cups	**grated Swiss cheese,** divided
12	**eggs**
2 cups	**milk**
I cup	**heavy cream**
I teaspoon	**dry mustard**
pinch of	**cayenne pepper**

Preheat oven to 400 degrees. Prepare a 12-cup Bundt pan with nonstick cooking spray.

In a large frying pan, saute spinach in oil over medium-high heat until wilted. Season with $^1/_2$ teaspoon salt, $^1/_4$ teaspoon pepper, and garlic. Remove to a small bowl and set aside to cool. In the same pan, fry hash browns until lightly browned and beginning to crisp. Season with salt and pepper. Set aside to cool.

In the prepared pan, layer half of bread cubes, then onions, spinach, hash browns, and half of cheese. Cover with remaining bread.

In a large bowl, whisk together eggs, milk, cream, remaining salt and pepper, mustard, and cayenne until completely mixed. Evenly pour over contents of pan, making sure the top is thoroughly wet. Press down lightly to settle contents into egg mixture and set aside for 30 minutes to soak up the liquid. Sprinkle remaining cheese over top, and bake for 40 minutes, or until a knife inserted in center comes out clean.

Allow to cool for 10 minutes then run a knife around the outside and inside edges and invert onto a serving platter. Makes 8–10 servings.

APPETIZERS & PARTY TREATS

PIMIENTO BUNOT
WITH BACON JAM

6 cups	**grated extra-sharp cheddar cheese**
1 1/4 pounds	**cream cheese,** softened
1 cup plus extra	**mayonnaise**
1/4 cup	**sour cream**
3/4 teaspoon	**garlic powder**
3/4 teaspoon	**cayenne pepper**
3/4 teaspoon	**onion powder**
1 1/2	**medium jalapeno peppers,** seeded and minced
1 can (12 ounces)	**diced pimientos,** drained
	salt and pepper, to taste
1–2 tablespoons	**Louisiana hot sauce,** or to taste, optional

Bacon Jam

1 pound	**black pepper bacon**
1 cup	**finely diced sweet onion**
1 tablespoon	**minced garlic**
1/4 cup	**firmly packed dark brown sugar**
6 ounces	**black coffee**
1/4 cup	**maple syrup**
1 1/2 tablespoons	**apple cider vinegar**
3 tablespoons	**balsamic vinegar**
1/2 teaspoon	**ground allspice**

Line a 12-cup Bundt pan with plastic wrap.

Place half the cheddar cheese into the large bowl of a mixer along with cream cheese, 1 cup mayonnaise, sour cream, garlic powder, cayenne, onion powder, jalapeno, and pimientos. Beat at medium speed with paddle attachment until thoroughly combined. Add remaining cheddar and more mayonnaise, if needed. Season with salt and pepper. Add hot sauce, if desired. Carefully pack the pan with the cheese spread. Refrigerate at least 3 hours or overnight.

For the jam, cut the bacon into 1-inch pieces and cook in a frying pan over medium-low heat, until almost crispy. Drain half the fat. Add the onion and garlic to the pan with remaining fat and cook until onions begin to caramelize, about 10 minutes. Add remaining ingredients. Reduce heat to simmer, cover, and cook for 30–45 minutes. Stir occasionally, adding water if mixture becomes too thick. When bacon is tender, remove from heat and cool for 30 minutes. Transfer bacon mixture to a food processor and pulse in batches to desired consistency.

When ready to serve, invert the cheese spread onto a serving plate and remove plastic wrap. Serve with warmed Bacon Jam. Makes 12 servings, or more for a party.

SAVORY GOAT CHEESE CHEESECAKE

²/₃ cup	**grated Parmesan cheese**
²/₃ cup	**panko breadcrumbs**
¹/₂ teaspoon	**garlic powder**
¹/₂ teaspoon plus more	**salt**
	pepper, to taste
2 tablespoons	**butter,** melted
8 ounces	**cream cheese,** softened
4 ounces	**soft goat cheese**
2	**eggs,** room temperature
¹/₄ cup	**sour cream**
¹/₄ cup	**jarred pesto**
	preserves of choice such as chutney, red onion jam, bacon jam, or other

Preheat oven to 350 degrees. Prepare a 12-cup Bundt or tube-style pan with nonstick cooking spray.

In a small bowl, stir together the cheese, breadcrumbs, garlic powder, a pinch of salt, and pepper. Mix in the butter until incorporated. Press mixture into the bottom of the pan.

In a large bowl, beat together the cream cheese and goat cheese until smooth and fluffy, 2–3 minutes. Add eggs, 1 at a time, mixing well after each addition. Add ¹/₂ teaspoon salt, sour cream, and pesto; mix until just incorporated. Pour filling into pan over crust. Bake for 40–50 minutes, or until center is set but still barely jiggly. Remove to a wire rack and cool for 30 minutes before inverting carefully onto a serving plate. Serve with preserves of choice. Makes 12 servings.

BACONY JALAPENO POPPERS

35	**jalapeno peppers,** halved lengthwise, stems, seeds, and ribs removed*
I package (8 ounces)	**grated Mexican four-cheese blend**
I package (8 ounces)	**grated Monterey Jack cheese**
I package (8 ounces)	**cream cheese,** cut up and softened
$1/2$ cup	**sour cream**
I teaspoon	**garlic powder**
$1/2$ teaspoon	**salt**
6 strips	**bacon,** cooked until crispy and crumbled
I tablespoon	**butter**
$1/3$ cup	**panko breadcrumbs**
$1/2$ teaspoon	**chili powder**

Preheat oven to 375 degrees. Prepare a 12-cup Bundt pan with nonstick cooking spray. Place the jalapenos, cut sides up, in the prepared pan.

In a medium bowl, beat together the grated cheeses, cream cheese, sour cream, garlic powder, and salt on low-to-medium speed until thoroughly combined. Add the bacon and stir to combine. Transfer mixture to a large resealable plastic bag, squeezing out excess air. Snip off one corner of the bag and pipe the mixture into the peppers.

Cover the pan with aluminum foil and bake for 45 minutes.

In a small frying pan, melt butter over medium heat. Stir in the breadcrumbs and chili powder. Cook for 2–3 minutes until crumbs are lightly toasted, stirring frequently. Remove pan from oven and sprinkle the toasted breadcrumbs over the stuffed peppers. Makes 12 servings.

*TIP: Wear rubber gloves when handling jalapeno or other fresh chile peppers to prevent skin from burning.

CHEESY PIMIENTO BUNDT

1 can (16.3 ounces)	**large refrigerated biscuits**
$^1/_2$ cup	**Palmetto Cheese spread,** any variety, or other pimiento cheese spread
$^1/_4$ cup	**grated cheddar cheese**

Preheat oven to 375 degrees. Prepare a 12-cup Bundt pan with nonstick cooking spray.

Lay the 8 biscuits flat on a lightly floured cutting board. Using a rolling pin, flatten the biscuits out a bit for more surface area.

Place 1 tablespoon of Palmetto Cheese into the center of one half of each biscuit. Fold the unfilled side over the filling and press firmly around the edges to seal. Place stuffed biscuits into the prepared pan and sprinkle the cheddar cheese over top. Bake for 40 minutes, or until biscuits are golden brown.

Remove from the oven and let cool for 10 minutes before inverting onto a serving platter. Makes 8 servings.

TUNA SALAD BUNDT

2 cans (11 ounces each)	**refrigerated French or Italian bread dough**
1/4 cup	**olive oil**
2 tablespoons	**Dijon mustard**
1 tablespoon	**fresh lemon juice**
1	**small shallot,** minced
1/2 teaspoon each	**salt and pepper**
2 cans (5 ounces each)	**chunk light tuna in water,** drained
1/2 cup	**grated cheddar cheese or Swiss cheese lettuce, tomato slices, red onion or other favorite toppings**

Preheat oven to 350 degrees. Prepare a 12-cup Bundt pan with nonstick cooking spray.

Place the rolled dough loaves into the bottom of the pan to form a ring, gently pinching the ends together. Bake for 30–35 minutes, or until golden brown. Remove to wire rack and allow to cool 15 minutes then carefully invert onto rack to completely cool. Slice the bread ring in half horizontally to make 2 layers and set each half, cut-side-up, on a baking sheet.

Turn oven to broil and lightly toast bread; remove and set aside.

In a small bowl, add the oil, mustard, lemon juice, shallot, and salt and pepper and whisk together until combined. Add tuna and mix together. Spread the tuna salad over the bottom bread ring. Sprinkle with the cheese and place under the broiler until cheese has melted.

Layer toppings of choice over the filling and add the top bread ring, slice and serve. Makes 10–12 servings.

CHICKEN SALAD BUNDT

2 cans (11 ounces each)	**refrigerated French or Italian bread dough**
$1/2$ cup plus 1 tablespoon	**mayonnaise,** divided
3 tablespoons	**Dijon mustard,** divided
$1/2$ teaspoon plus a pinch	**salt**
$1/2$ teaspoon plus a pinch	**pepper**
3 cups	**shredded rotisserie or leftover roasted chicken**
$1/2$ cup	**finely diced celery**
$1/2$ cup	**chopped pecans**
	lettuce, tomato slices, red onion, or other favorite toppings

Preheat oven to 350 degrees. Prepare a 12-cup Bundt pan with nonstick cooking spray.

Place the rolled dough loaves into the bottom of the pan to form a ring, gently pinching the ends together. Bake for 30–35 minutes, or until golden brown. Remove to wire rack and allow to cool 15 minutes then carefully invert onto rack to completely cool.

Slice the bread ring in half horizontally to make 2 layers. Spread 1 tablespoon mayonnaise over the cut side of 1 of the bread halves and 1 tablespoon mustard over the other. Sprinkle each half with a pinch of salt and pepper.

In a large bowl, combine remaining mayonnaise, mustard, salt, and pepper. Stir in chicken, celery, and pecans until mixed well. Spread the chicken salad evenly over the bottom bread ring. Layer toppings of choice over the chicken salad. Add the top bread ring, slice, and serve. Makes 10–12 servings.

MEATBALL-STUFFED BREAD

2 cans (11 ounces each)	**refrigerated French bread dough**
4 tablespoons	**butter**
1/2 teaspoon	**garlic powder**
24	**small frozen Italian meatballs,** thawed and warmed
3/4 cup	**marinara sauce,** warmed
6 slices	**provolone cheese,** halved

Preheat oven to 350 degrees. Prepare a 12-cup fluted tube pan with nonstick cooking spray. Line an 13 x 18-inch baking sheet with parchment paper.

Place the rolled dough loaves into the bottom of the pan to form a ring, gently pinching the ends together. Bake for 30–35 minutes, or until golden brown. Remove to wire rack and allow to cool 15 minutes then carefully invert onto rack to completely cool. Do not turn oven off.

Slice the bread ring in half horizontally to make 2 layers. Pinch or tear bread from cut sides of top and bottom halves, leaving about a 3/4-inch shell; discard or save bread pieces for another use, such as fresh breadcrumbs. Place bread rings cut side up on the baking sheet.

Place the butter and garlic powder in a small microwave-safe bowl and microwave for 30 seconds, or until melted. Brush hollowed out sides of each ring with garlic butter.

Combine warmed meatballs and sauce together in a bowl. Arrange cheese slice halves inside the top bread ring and spread meatball mixture inside the bottom bread ring. Bake for 8–12 minutes, or until cheese is melted and rings are hot. Carefully top the meatball ring with the cheese ring. Slice to serve. Makes 8 servings.

SANGRIA ICE MOLD

1	**orange,** thinly sliced
1	**lemon,** thinly sliced
1 cup	**pineapple chunks**
$^1/_4$ cup	**pomegranate seeds**
$^1/_2$ cup	**pomegranate juice**
2 cups	**orange juice**
	wine, optional
	triple sec, optional
	fresh fruit slices, optional

Prepare a 12-cup Bundt pan with nonstick cooking spray and line with plastic wrap.

Carefully arrange the fruit in a decorative pattern around the pan. Slowly pour the juices over the fruit. Tuck pan into the freezer for at least 6 hours.

Unmold into punch bowl, remove plastic wrap, and add your favorite sangria ingredients, such as wine, triple sec, and fruit slices.

HOLIDAY ICE MOLD

I	**orange,** thinly sliced
I cup	**fresh cranberries**
I cup	**cranberry juice**
I cup	**orange juice**
I liter	**ginger ale**
4 sprigs	**rosemary,** optional

Prepare a 12-cup Bundt pan with nonstick cooking spray and line with plastic wrap.

Carefully arrange the fruit in a decorative pattern around the pan. Slowly pour the juices and ginger ale over the fruit. For the holidays, you may want to add rosemary. Tuck pan into the freezer for at least 6 hours.

Unmold into punch bowl, remove plastic wrap, and add your favorite punch ingredients.

MOJITO ICE MOLD

2	**limes,** thinly sliced
1 bunch	**mint**
4 cups	**ginger ale or water**

Prepare a 12-cup Bundt pan with nonstick cooking spray and line with plastic wrap.

Carefully arrange the limes and mint leaves in a decorative pattern around the pan. Slowly pour the ginger ale over the top. Tuck pan into the freezer for at least 6 hours.

Unmold into punch bowl, remove plastic wrap, and add your favorite mojito ingredients.

SIDE DISHES

POTATO SALAD BUNDT

1 cup	**mayonnaise**
1 tablespoon	**white wine vinegar**
1 tablespoon	**Dijon mustard**
	salt and pepper, to taste
3	**hard-boiled eggs,** chopped
7 cups	**diced cooked potatoes**
1 cup	**finely diced celery**
1/4 cup	**sliced green onions**
1 package (9 ounces)	**frozen baby peas,** thawed and drained on paper towels

Prepare a 12-cup Bundt or tube pan with nonstick cooking spray. Line with plastic wrap.

In a large bowl, combine the mayonnaise, vinegar, mustard, and salt and pepper. Gently stir the eggs, potatoes, celery, and onions into dressing mixture.

Carefully pack half of the potato salad into the pan, top with the peas, and then finish with the remaining potato salad. Cover and refrigerate for at least 4 hours, or overnight. Carefully invert onto a serving platter and remove plastic wrap. Makes 12 servings.

MACARONI AND CHEESE BUNDT

I cup	**fresh breadcrumbs,** divided
5 tablespoons	**butter,** melted, divided
3 cups	**grated sharp cheddar cheese,** divided
$^1/_4$ teaspoon	**garlic powder**
$^1/_2$ tablespoon	**dry mustard**
I teaspoon	**sea salt**
$^1/_2$ teaspoon	**pepper**
I $^1/_2$ cups	**whole milk**
I cup	**half-and-half**
4	**egg whites,** lightly beaten
I cup	**grated Mexican-style cheese blend**
8 ounces	**elbow macaroni,** cooked, hot

Preheat oven to 350 degrees. Prepare a 12-cup Bundt pan with nonstick cooking spray.

Combine $^1/_3$ cup breadcrumbs, I tablespoon butter, and I cup cheddar cheese. Line the bottom of the pan with the cheese mixture.

In a large bowl, mix remaining butter, remaining breadcrumbs, garlic powder, mustard, salt, and pepper. Whisk in the milk, half-and-half, and egg whites; thoroughly combine. Add in the remaining cheddar cheese and the Mexican-style cheese; stir to combine. Fold in the macaroni while it is still hot; the heat will help to melt and incorporate the mixture. Pour into prepared pan.

Bake for I hour. Cool for 15 minutes. Carefully invert onto a serving platter. Makes 8–10 servings.

RIGATONI BUNDT

Topping

$1/2$ loaf	**stale French or Italian bread,** cubed
1 sprig	**rosemary**
6	**fresh basil leaves**
3–4	**fresh sage leaves**
$1/2$ cup	**Parmesan cheese**
$1/2$ teaspoon each	**salt and pepper**
4 tablespoons	**butter,** melted, divided

Rigatoni

4 tablespoons	**butter**
$1/4$ cup	**flour**
4 cups	**milk,** warm
1 teaspoon each	**salt and pepper**
2 tablespoons	**Dijon mustard**
2 cups	**grated cheddar cheese**
1 cup	**grated Swiss cheese**
$1/2$ cup	**grated Parmesan cheese**
1 pound	**mezzi rigatoni,** cooked and drained

Preheat oven to 350 degrees. Prepare a 12-cup Bundt pan with nonstick cooking spray. In a food processor, pulse dry topping ingredients until the consistency of breadcrumbs. Sprinkle 1/2 cup topping into the prepared pan and drizzle with 2 tablespoons butter.

For the rigatoni, melt butter in a large saucepan over medium heat. Just before it begins to brown, add the flour. Whisk and cook for 2–3 minutes. Add milk, slowly whisking to incorporate. Add the salt, pepper, and mustard and simmer until the sauce thickens; whisking constantly. Stir in the cheeses. Once cheeses are melted and combined, add pasta and mix thoroughly. Transfer pasta mixture to the prepared pan. Sprinkle with 1/2 cup topping and drizzle the remaining melted butter over top.

Bake for 30–40 minutes, until bubbly. Allow to rest for 10–15 minutes before carefully inverting onto a serving platter. Makes 8–10 servings.

PASTA SALAD WITH CRUDITE

3 cups	**dry elbow macaroni**
1/4 cup	**mayonnaise**
1 package (8 ounces)	**cream cheese,** room temperature
1/4 cup	**sweet pickle relish**
1/4 cup	**finely chopped fresh parsley,** plus more for garnish
1 tablespoon	**Dijon mustard**
1 cup	**chopped cucumber,** plus more for garnish
1/2 cup	**chopped celery**
1/2 cup	**sliced radishes,** plus more for garnish
1/2 teaspoon	**salt**

Prepare a 12-cup Bundt or tube pan with nonstick cooking spray. Line with plastic wrap.

Prepare the macaroni according to package directions. Drain and set aside; keep hot.

In a large bowl, mix together the mayonnaise, cream cheese, relish, parsley, and mustard. While the macaroni is still hot, mix it into the mayonnaise mixture and combine completely. Add the cucumber, celery, radishes, and salt.

Spoon into the pan and lightly push on the salad to form into the pan shape; refrigerate for at least 3 hours until firm. Carefully invert pan onto a serving platter and remove the plastic wrap. Sprinkle parsley over the top and garnish sides with extra parsley, cucumber, and radish. Makes 12 servings.

A tube pan works best for these types of salads.

SWEET POTATO CASSEROLE

Topping

1 cup	**firmly packed light brown sugar**
$^1/_2$ cup	**flour**
1 cup	**chopped pecans**
4 tablespoons	**butter,** softened

Casserole

10 tablespoons	**butter,** softened, divided
$^1/_2$ cup	**dry stuffing cubes,** processed into crumbs
5 cups	**cubed sweet potatoes,** cooked and mashed
$^1/_2$ cup	**sugar**
$^1/_2$ cup	**firmly packed light brown sugar**
1 teaspoon	**ground cinnamon**
$^1/_2$ cup	**whole milk**
3	**eggs**
	mini marshmallows, optional

Preheat oven to 350 degrees. To make the topping, mix together the brown sugar, flour, pecans, and butter; set aside.

Generously coat the inside of a 12-cup Bundt pan with 2 tablespoons butter. Sprinkle stuffing crumbs into the bottom and sides of the pan. Spread topping mixture evenly onto the bottom of the pan.

In a large bowl, combine the sweet potatoes, sugar, brown sugar, cinnamon, remaining butter, milk, and eggs; mix well. Pour mixture over the topping.

Bake for 30 minutes. Remove from oven and allow to rest for 20 minutes before inverting carefully onto a serving platter. If desired, sprinkle with mini marshmallows. Makes 10–12 servings.

CHEDDAR-ONION BREAD STUFFING

5 tablespoons	**butter,** divided
3 tablespoons	**olive oil**
5	**onions,** halved and thinly sliced
	salt, to taste
12 slices	**sourdough bread,** lightly toasted and cut into 1-inch cubes
	pepper, to taste
2 tablespoons	**fresh thyme**
1/2 pound	**cheddar cheese,** grated
2	**eggs,** whisked
1 cup	**beef stock,** heated

Preheat oven to 375 degrees. Prepare a 12-cup Bundt pan with nonstick baking spray.

In a large frying pan, melt 3 tablespoons of butter and add the oil. Add the onions and saute for 5 minutes. Sprinkle with salt and stir, allowing the onions to caramelize slowly for 30–45 minutes. Set aside.

Place the bread in a large bowl. Melt the remaining butter and drizzle over the bread. Season with salt and pepper. Add the thyme, cheese, eggs, and onions; toss to combine. Add the stock and stir gently to moisten all the ingredients.

Pour the mixture into the prepared pan; cover with aluminum foil. Bake for 30 minutes then remove the foil and continue baking until golden brown, about 25 more minutes. Makes 10–12 servings.

MACARONI AND CHEESE WITH GARLIC BREADCRUMBS

1 cup	**garlic breadcrumbs,** divided
1/2 cup	**grated Parmesan cheese**
2 tablespoons	**butter**
1/4 cup	**flour**
2 cups	**whole milk**
3	**eggs,** beaten
1/2 teaspoon	**dry mustard**
1/2 teaspoon	**garlic powder**
1/2 teaspoon	**onion powder**
20 ounces	**sharp cheddar cheese,** grated
1 pound	**macaroni,** cooked al dente

Preheat oven to 400 degrees. Generously prepare a 12-cup Bundt pan with nonstick cooking spray.

Mix together 1/4 cup breadcrumbs and Parmesan cheese. Pour crumbs into the prepared pan and shake until all sides are coated with the mixture.

Place the butter in a saucepan over medium heat. Once the butter starts melting, whisk in the flour. Then whisk quickly while pouring in the milk to break up the flour clumps. Whisk quickly again to incorporate the eggs into the milk mixture without scrambling them. Whisk in the mustard, garlic powder, and onion powder. Add the cheddar cheese and stir until melted into the mixture. Add the pasta, stirring until combined. Add the remaining breadcrumbs and stir to thoroughly coat the pasta.

Spoon into the prepared pan and bake for 30–40 minutes, until crisp around the edges and bubbly. Cool for 15 minutes in the pan. Run a long, thin spatula around the edges and down the sides. Invert onto a serving platter. Serve warm or at room temperature. Makes 10 servings.

SCALLOPED POTATO DUO

1 package (14 ounces)	**refrigerated pie crusts**
1 tablespoon	**finely chopped fresh rosemary or thyme**
1/4 teaspoon	**pepper**
1/4 teaspoon	**ground cinnamon**
8 ounces	**Gruyere cheese,** grated, divided
1 1/2 pounds	**Yukon gold potatoes**
1 1/2 pounds	**sweet potatoes**
	salt, to taste
2/3 cup	**heavy cream**
1 clove	**garlic,** minced

Preheat oven to 450 degrees. Prepare a 12-cup Bundt pan with nonstick cooking spray.

Unroll pie crusts on a lightly floured surface. Sprinkle rosemary, pepper, cinnamon, and 1/2 cup cheese over 1 pie crust; top with remaining crust. With a small, round cookie cutter (or knife) cut a 4-inch hole in the center. Place the crusts into the prepared pan, pressing the crust down and onto the sides. Chill in the refrigerator while you peel and thinly slice the potatoes.

Layer one-third each of Yukon gold potatoes, sweet potatoes, and salt in prepared crust. Sprinkle with 1/4 cup cheese. Repeat layers twice, pressing layers down slightly to fit.

Warm the cream and garlic in a 1-cup microwave-safe measuring cup for 30 seconds; pour over potato layers in pan. Sprinkle with remaining cheese. Cover pan with aluminum foil. Place on a baking sheet.

Bake for 1 hour. Remove foil and bake for 20 minutes, or until potatoes are soft and crust is browned. Allow to rest for 10–15 minutes. Carefully invert onto a serving plate. Makes 8–10 servings.

BACON-WRAPPED LOADED MASHED POTATOES

2 tablespoons	**butter,** melted
28 slices	**bacon** (or more)
3 tablespoons	**barbecue sauce**
4 cups	**leftover mashed potatoes**
I cup	**grated cheddar cheese**
4	**scallions,** thinly sliced
	salt and pepper, to taste
¹/₂ cup	**sour cream**

Preheat oven to 400 degrees. Prepare a 12-cup Bundt pan by brushing the butter carefully into every crevice.

Line the pan with slices of bacon, slightly overlapping. Use a pastry brush to spread a thin coating of barbecue sauce on the inside of the bacon.

In a large bowl, mix the mashed potatoes, cheese, scallions, salt and pepper, and sour cream together. Carefully scoop the potato mixture into the pan. Fold over any hanging bacon onto the potato mixture.

Bake for 30 minutes, until bacon is cooked completely. Remove from oven and allow to rest for 10 minutes before inverting onto a serving platter. Makes 12–14 servings.

STUFFED SPINACH AND ARTICHOKE BREAD

1 1/4 cups	**freshly grated Parmesan cheese,** divided
1 can (11 ounces)	**refrigerated bread dough** (Italian or French)
1/2 cup	**sour cream**
1/2 cup	**mayonnaise**
8 ounces	**cream cheese,** room temperature
1/2 cup	**frozen spinach,** thawed and liquid squeezed out
1 can (14 ounces)	**artichoke hearts,** drained and chopped
1 clove	**garlic,** minced

Preheat oven to 350 degrees. Generously prepare a 12-cup Bundt pan with nonstick cooking spray. Sprinkle 1/4 cup Parmesan cheese around the inside of the pan.

Remove bread dough from the can. Roll it out on a lightly floured work surface until roughly 1/2 inch thick. Using a cutter or a knife, cut out a 4-inch circle in the center of the dough and fit it over the center column of the pan. Line the bottom of the pan, placing the dough so that there is enough lip around the inner column and outer edge of the pan to fold together after adding the filling.

In a large bowl, combine the sour cream, mayonnaise, cream cheese, spinach, artichokes, garlic, and remaining Parmesan cheese. Mix together until smooth. Scoop the spinach mixture into the bread tunnel. Pinch the ends of the dough together so that the seam is closer to the middle column.

Bake for about 30 minutes until bread is evenly browned. Remove from oven and allow to rest for 10 minutes before carefully inverting onto a serving platter. Makes 8–10 servings.

SPICY POTATO-STUFFED NAAN BUNDT

Bread

2 tablespoons	**yeast**
I tablespoon	**warm water**
I tablespoon plus I teaspoon	**sugar,** divided
3 cups	**flour**
I teaspoon	**salt**
7 tablespoons	**powdered milk**
3/4 cup	**milk,** warm
1/4 cup	**heavy cream**
2 tablespoons	**canola oil,** divided

Potatoes

3	**russet potatoes,** diced into I-inch cubes
	salt and pepper, to taste
I teaspoon	**garam masala**
I tablespoon	**chopped fresh cilantro**
I tablespoon	**fresh mint leaves**
I clove	**garlic,** minced
I teaspoon	**lemon juice**
3 tablespoons	**melted butter plus more as needed,** for brushing

In a small bowl, combine the yeast with the water and I teaspoon sugar. Let rest for 5 minutes. In another bowl, combine the flour, salt, remaining sugar, and powdered milk. Mix well.

Make a well in the center of the dry ingredients. Add the warm milk, cream, 1 tablespoon oil, and the yeast mixture. Mix well. Place the dough onto a flat, lightly floured surface and knead well for at least 5 minutes. Add the remaining 1 tablespoon oil and knead well for several additional minutes until the dough is soft and smooth. Cover the dough and keep in a warm place for about 1 hour.

Meanwhile, boil the potatoes until tender, smash them gently (you want them chunky), and season with salt, pepper, and garam masala. With a small mortar and pestle, grind the cilantro, mint, garlic, and lemon juice into a paste. Stir into potato mixture.

Prepare a 12-cup Bundt pan with nonstick baking spray.

Punch down the dough and knead for about 1 minute. Form round balls about 3 inches in diameter then flatten them to about $^1/_2$ inch thick. Divide potato mixture evenly among the dough circles, form the dough into a ball around the potatoes, and place the balls in the prepared pan. Allow to proof again until almost double in size about 30 minutes.

Preheat oven to 350 degrees.

Brush the dough with the butter, cover the pan with aluminum foil, and bake for 10 minutes. Remove foil and continue to bake uncovered for 20 additional minutes until browned. Check for doneness and remove from oven. Brush with additional butter and serve. Makes 8–10 servings.

ROASTED VEGETABLES

2 tablespoons **olive oil**
4 cloves **garlic,** minced
salt and pepper, to taste
2 cups **fresh broccoli florets**
1 **zucchini,** quartered and sliced
1 **yellow squash,** quartered and sliced
1 **red bell pepper,** chopped
1 **red onion,** chopped

Preheat oven to 400 degrees. Prepare a 12-cup Bundt pan with nonstick cooking spray.

In a small bowl, mix the oil, garlic, and salt and pepper.

Place all the vegetables in the prepared pan, drizzle with the oil mixture, and toss. Bake for 15 minutes, until vegetables are crisp-tender. Makes 6 servings.

DINNERS

TURKEY MEATLOAF WITH CRANBERRY SAUCE

I can (16 ounces)	**whole cranberry sauce**
2 teaspoons	**Dijon mustard,** divided
2 tablespoons	**firmly packed brown sugar**
I pound	**ground turkey**
1 1/2 cups	**panko breadcrumbs**
I	**medium onion,** finely chopped
1/3 cup	**milk**
I	**egg**
1/2 teaspoon	**salt**
	pepper, to taste
1/4 teaspoon	**finely minced fresh parsley**
1/4 teaspoon	**finely minced fresh thyme**
1/4 teaspoon	**finely minced fresh sage**

Preheat oven to 375 degrees. Prepare a 6-cup Bundt pan with nonstick cooking spray.

In a small bowl, stir together the cranberry sauce, I teaspoon mustard, and the brown sugar. Set aside.

In a large bowl, combine the turkey, breadcrumbs, onion, milk, egg, salt, pepper, parsley, thyme, sage, and remaining mustard. Shape meat into the prepared pan.

Bake, uncovered, for 30 minutes. Spread 1/2 cup cranberry mixture on top of loaf. Bake for 20–30 minutes more, until meatloaf reaches an internal temperature of 165 degrees.

Heat remaining cranberry mixture in a small pan over low heat until heated through. Serve with meatloaf. Makes 6–8 servings.

CHEESE-FILLED ITALIAN CHICKEN MEATLOAF

1 1/2 pounds	**ground chicken**
1 1/2 cups	**panko breadcrumbs**
1	**medium onion,** chopped
1/4 cup	**jarred sun-dried tomatoes,** drained
1/3 cup	**milk**
1	**egg**
1 teaspoon	**Dijon mustard**
1/2 teaspoon	**salt**
	pepper, to taste
1 tablespoon	**finely minced fresh Italian parsley**
1/2 cup	**grated Pecorino Romano cheese**
1 1/2 cups	**grated Italian cheese blend**
1 1/2 cups	**marinara sauce,** divided, plus more for serving

Preheat oven to 375 degrees. Prepare a 12-cup Bundt pan with nonstick cooking spray.

In a large bowl, combine all the ingredients except the Italian cheese and marinara. Place two-thirds of the meatloaf mix into the prepared pan, carving a small tunnel in the middle.

In a medium bowl, combine the Italian cheese and 1/2 cup of the marinara sauce. Transfer the mixture into the tunnel. Top with the remaining meatloaf mixture. Bake, uncovered, for 30 minutes. Remove from oven and top the meatloaf with remaining marinara sauce. Bake for 20–30 minutes more, until meatloaf reaches an internal temperature of 165 degrees. Serve with additional marinara, if desired. Makes 8–10 servings.

GREEK-STYLE SHEPHERD'S PIE

3 cups	**leftover mashed potatoes**
1	**egg**
$^1/_2$ cup	**tomato sauce**
1 teaspoon	**brown sugar**
$^1/_2$ teaspoon	**dried oregano**
1 tablespoon	**Worcestershire sauce**
2 pounds	**ground lamb**
$^1/_2$ cup	**chopped onion**
1 clove	**garlic,** minced
8 ounces	**mushrooms,** of choice, sliced
1 cup	**sour cream**
2 tablespoons	**prepared mustard** (preferably grainy mustard)

Preheat oven to 400 degrees. Prepare a 12-cup Bundt pan with nonstick cooking spray.

In a large bowl, stir together the potatoes and egg; mix well. Using the back of a spoon, press 2$^1/_2$ cups of potatoes into the bottom and three-fourths of the way up the sides of the prepared pan. Reserve remaining potatoes.

In a small bowl, combine the tomato sauce, brown sugar, oregano, and Worcestershire sauce; set aside.

In a large skillet over medium-high heat, cook the lamb, onion, garlic, and mushrooms until browned; drain well. Stir in the reserved potatoes, sour cream, tomato sauce mixture, and mustard. Spoon into the potato-lined pan.

Bake for 30–35 minutes. Cool on a wire rack for 10 minutes before inverting onto a serving platter. Makes 6–8 servings.

STROGANOFF-STYLE SHEPHERD'S PIE

3 cups	**leftover mashed potatoes**
1	**egg**
1/2 cup	**tomato sauce**
1 teaspoon	**brown sugar**
1 tablespoon	**Worcestershire sauce**
2 pounds	**ground beef**
1/2 cup	**chopped onion**
1 clove	**garlic,** minced
8 ounces	**mushrooms,** of choice, sliced
1 cup	**sour cream**
2 tablespoons	**prepared mustard** (preferably grainy mustard)

Preheat oven to 400 degrees. Prepare a 12-cup Bundt pan with nonstick cooking spray.

In a large bowl, stir together the potatoes and egg; mix well. Using the back of a spoon, press 2 1/4 cups of the potatoes into the bottom and three-fourths of the way up the sides of the prepared pan. Reserve remaining potatoes.

In a small bowl, combine the tomato sauce, brown sugar, and Worcestershire sauce; set aside.

In a large skillet over medium-high heat, cook the beef, onion, garlic, and mushrooms until browned; drain well. Stir in reserved potatoes, tomato sauce mixture, sour cream, and mustard. Spoon into the potato-lined pan.

Bake for 30–35 minutes. Cool on a wire rack for 10 minutes before inverting onto a serving platter. Makes 6–8 servings.

ROAST CHICKEN DINNER

3 cloves	**garlic**
3	**carrots,** chopped
1	**onion,** quartered
1 pound	**Yukon gold potatoes,** quartered
	sliced fennel, optional
	sliced parsnips, optional
	extra virgin olive oil
	salt and pepper, to taste
1	**large bunch thyme**
1	**large bunch rosemary**
1	**chicken** (4 pounds), gizzards removed
1	**lemon,** halved

Preheat oven to 425 degrees. Cover the hole of a 12-cup Bundt pan with aluminum foil. Spray the pan with nonstick cooking spray.

In the pan, combine the garlic, carrots, onion, potatoes, fennel, and parsnips. Toss with oil to coat and season with salt and pepper. Place a few sprigs of thyme and rosemary on top of the vegetables.

Pat the chicken dry with paper towels. Season the inside of the cavity generously with salt and pepper, and then stuff it with the lemon halves and a few sprigs of thyme and rosemary. Rub oil all over the skin of the chicken then season generously with salt and pepper.

Straddle the chicken over the middle of the pan, breast side up. Bake until the chicken is cooked through and skin is golden, 60–70 minutes. Let chicken rest for at least 15 minutes before slicing. Serve with roasted vegetables and pan juices. Makes 4–6 servings.

VARIATION: For extra special pan juices, pour juices into a small saucepan and bring to boil. Add $1/2$ cup white wine and 2 tablespoons butter and allow to simmer for a few minutes. Finish off with a sprinkling of parsley. Pour over chicken and vegetables or serve on the side.

DAY-AFTER-THANKSGIVING IN A BUNDT

6 cups	**cubed dry bread,** divided
2¹/₂ cups	**diced cooked turkey**
2 cups	**grated Swiss cheese**
I	**small onion,** diced and sauteed in butter
3 cups	**leftover mashed potatoes**
4	**eggs,** beaten
2¹/₂ cups	**milk**
¹/₄ teaspoon	**pepper**
I¹/₂ tablespoons	**minced fresh herbs** (such as Italian parsley, sage, and thyme)
	leftover gravy, optional
	leftover cranberry sauce, optional

Preheat oven to 350 degrees. Prepare a 12-cup Bundt pan with nonstick cooking spray.

Spread 3 cups of the bread cubes in the bottom of the prepared pan. Arrange the turkey evenly over bread. Sprinkle the cheese over top. Sprinkle with onion. Spoon the potatoes over all. Top with remaining bread cubes.

In a large bowl, combine the eggs with the milk, pepper, and herbs; pour over the mixture in the pan.

Set the pan inside a large casserole dish or a roasting pan and add hot water to the larger pan to make a water bath. Bake for I hour. Remove from water bath and cook for an additional 10 minutes, or until a knife comes out clean. Remove from oven and allow to rest for 10 minutes before carefully inverting onto a serving platter. Serve with leftover gravy and cranberry sauce, if desired. Makes 6–8 servings.

CACIO E PEPE SPAGHETTI BUNDT

5 tablespoons	**butter,** melted
1/2 cup plus 1 tablespoon	**grated Pecorino Romano cheese,** divided
1 pound	**dry spaghetti**
2 cups	**grated mozzarella cheese**
3/4 cup	**grated Parmigiano-Reggiano cheese**
1 1/2 cups	**whole milk**
3	**eggs,** beaten
2 teaspoons	**salt**
3 teaspoons	**pepper**

Preheat oven to 425 degrees. Prepare a 12-cup Bundt pan by brushing with 2 tablespoons melted butter and then sprinkling with 1 tablespoon of the Pecorino Romano cheese.

Bring a large pot of salted water to a boil and cook spaghetti until al dente. Drain well.

Place spaghetti in a large bowl and toss with the remaining Pecorino Romano, mozzarella, and Parmigiano-Reggiano cheeses. Add the milk, eggs, remaining butter, salt, and, pepper and toss to combine. Pour into the prepared pan. The pepper makes this dish—so the more the better.

Bake until cheese is melted and bubbling, 35–40 minutes. Set on a wire rack to cool for 15 minutes before inverting onto a serving platter. Makes 6–8 servings.

CHICKEN ENCHILADA CASSEROLE

1 tablespoon	**vegetable oil**
1 cup	**diced onions**
2 cloves	**garlic,** minced
1 teaspoon	**taco seasoning**
1 1/2 cups	**shredded rotisserie chicken**
2 cups	**grated Mexican cheese blend,** divided
2 boxes (8.5 ounces each)	**cornbread mix**
2/3 cup	**milk**
3	**eggs**
1/2 cup	**prepared enchilada sauce,** warmed
	sliced scallions, for garnish
	jalapenos, optional
	sour cream, optional

Preheat oven to 400 degrees. Prepare a 12-cup Bundt pan with nonstick cooking spray.

In a large frying pan, heat oil over medium. Saute onions until softened, about 5 minutes. Stir in the garlic, cooking for 1 minute. Stir in taco seasoning, allowing to bloom for about 30 seconds. Add the chicken, stirring to mix well. Remove from heat. Stir in 1 1/2 cups of cheese.

In a large bowl, prepare the cornbread batter by whisking together the mix with the milk and eggs. Pour half of the batter into the prepared pan. Spoon the meat mixture into the middle of the pan on top of the cornbread batter. Cover the meat filling with the remaining batter, making sure the filling is completely covered.

Bake for 30–35 minutes, until the cornbread is browned on top and a toothpick inserted into the cornbread comes out free of crumbs.

Cool for 5 minutes before inverting onto a serving plate. Pour the enchilada sauce over the top, sprinkle with the remaining cheese, and garnish with the scallions before slicing. Serve with jalapenos and sour cream, if desired. Makes 8–10 servings.

LEMONY CHICKEN DINNER

3	**medium carrots,** peeled and cut into 2-inch pieces
2	**russet potatoes,** cut into 1-inch chunks
1	**medium onion,** quartered
1 tablespoon	**minced garlic**
6 tablespoons	**olive oil,** divided
	salt and pepper, to taste
1 handful	**thyme sprigs**
1	**lemon,** sliced into rounds
6	**chicken thighs,** bone in and skin on
	red pepper flakes, to taste

Preheat oven to 425 degrees. Prepare a 12-cup Bundt pan with nonstick cooking spray.

Add the carrots, potatoes, onion, garlic, and 2 tablespoons of the oil to pan. Season with salt and pepper. Mix well.

Top the vegetables with a layer of thyme then a layer of lemon slices. Season the chicken with salt and pepper; transfer chicken, skin side up, to pan. Brush chicken with the remaining oil and sprinkle with red pepper. Bake uncovered for 35–45 minutes until chicken reaches a temperature of 165 degrees. Makes 4–6 servings.

VARIATION: For a delicious twist, you may also mix together the ingredients for a boxed stuffing mix and place on the bottom of the pan before putting in the vegetables.

DOUBLE CORNBREAD-
STUFFED WITH CHILI

I cup	**self-rising white cornmeal mix**
1/2 cup	**self-rising flour,** sifted
1/4 cup	**corn muffin mix**
2 tablespoons	**sugar**
2	**eggs,** beaten
I can (15 ounces)	**cream-style corn**
I cup	**buttermilk**
I 1/2 cups	**leftover chili**
1/2 cup	**grated cheddar cheese**
	Fritos, optional
	sour cream, optional
	chopped onions, optional

Preheat oven to 400 degrees. Prepare a 12-cup Bundt pan with nonstick baking spray.

In a medium bowl, combine the cornmeal mix, flour, corn muffin mix, sugar, eggs, corn, and buttermilk. Stir until smooth and pourable. Small lumps are okay. Set aside.

Place empty pan in hot oven for 5 minutes. Remove carefully from oven and spread half the batter into the pan. Carefully spoon chili on top of batter, top with cheese, and then finish off with the rest of the batter.

Reduce oven to 350 degrees. Bake for 25–30 minutes, until browned and the top is firm. Remove from oven and cool on a wire rack for 10 minutes before inverting onto a serving plate. Serve with chili fixings (Fritos, sour cream, onions). Makes 8 servings.

PATTY MELT CASSEROLE

I tablespoon	**vegetable oil**
2	**yellow onions,** diced
2 teaspoons	**sugar**
I cup	**mayonnaise**
$^1/_2$ cup	**ketchup**
4 tablespoons	**minced dill pickles,** divided
I $^1/_2$ pounds	**ground beef**
I tablespoon	**Worcestershire sauce**
I tablespoon	**minced garlic**
2 teaspoons	**pepper**
I teaspoon	**salt**
I teaspoon	**caraway seeds**
2 tablespoons	**flour**
I cup	**low-sodium beef broth**
2 cans (16.3 ounces each)	**large refrigerated biscuits**
12 ounces	**Swiss cheese,** grated

Preheat oven to 400 degrees. Prepare a 12-cup Bundt pan with nonstick cooking spray.

In a frying pan over medium heat, add the oil then the onions and sugar. Cook, covered, for 20–25 minutes, until caramelized. Meanwhile, whisk together the mayonnaise, ketchup, and 2 tablespoons of the pickles. Set aside.

Add the beef, Worcestershire sauce, garlic, pepper, salt, and caraway seeds to the frying pan with the onions. Increase heat to high and cook, stirring frequently and breaking meat into small pieces, until meat is browned. Drain and discard all but 2 tablespoons of drippings.

Stir in the flour and cook for 3 minutes over medium-high heat. Stir in the broth and 1 cup of the mayonnaise mixture; cook to thicken into gravy.

Line the bottom and sides of the prepared pan with the biscuits from 1 can and spread 4 ounces of the cheese on top of the biscuits. Top with the meat mixture, spreading evenly, and 6 ounces of the cheese. Cover this mixture with the biscuits from the second can.

Bake for 20–25 minutes until biscuits are lightly browned. Allow to rest for 10 minutes before inverting onto a serving platter. Sprinkle remaining 2 ounces cheese over top. Drizzle the casserole with some of the mayonnaise mixture and remaining pickles. Serve remaining dressing on the side. Makes 6–8 servings.

GENERAL TSO'S CHICKEN

4	**large potatoes,** peeled and cut into 3-inch pieces
	salt and pepper, to taste
2 teaspoons	**sesame oil**
1 clove	**garlic,** minced
1 inch	**fresh ginger,** minced
1 tablespoon	**minced green onions**
2 tablespoons	**orange zest**
2 tablespoons	**rice vinegar**
$1/2$ cup	**soy sauce**
$1/4$ cup	**water**
1 tablespoon	**cornstarch**
$1/4$ cup	**honey**
1 teaspoon	**peanut butter**
3 teaspoons	**chili paste**
1 teaspoon	**olive oil**
6	**chicken thighs**

Preheat oven to 450 degrees. Prepare a 12-cup Bundt pan with nonstick cooking spray. Lay the potatoes in the bottom of the pan then sprinkle with salt and pepper.

In a medium saucepan over medium-low heat, warm the sesame oil. Add the garlic, ginger, green onions, and orange zest. Saute for 2 minutes. Whisk in the rice vinegar and soy sauce. In a small cup, whisk together the water and cornstarch then add it to the pan. Whisk in the honey, peanut butter, chili paste, and oil. Reduce heat to low and stir occasionally until the sauce has thickened. Set aside.

Season chicken with salt and pepper and arrange over potatoes. Drizzle half the sauce over chicken. Bake for 40 minutes, or until chicken and potatoes are cooked through. Remove from oven and drizzle remaining sauce over chicken. Makes 4–6 servings.

ITALIAN CHICKEN

6	**chicken thighs**
2 teaspoons	**salt**
I teaspoon	**pepper**
I	**large red bell pepper,** chopped
4	**carrots,** cut into 3-inch pieces
I	**onion,** chopped
3 cloves	**garlic,** finely chopped
I can (28 ounces)	**diced tomatoes**
3/4 cup	**reduced-sodium chicken broth**
3/4 cup	**dry white wine**
2 tablespoons	**Italian seasoning blend**
2 tablespoons	**olive oil**

Preheat oven to 400 degrees. Prepare a 12-cup Bundt pan with nonstick cooking spray.

Sprinkle the chicken with salt and pepper. Line the bottom of the pan with the bell pepper, carrots, onion, garlic, tomatoes, broth, and wine. Arrange the chicken thighs on top of the vegetables; sprinkle with the Italian seasoning and oil.

Bake for 40–45 minutes, until the chicken is cooked through. Remove from oven, place the chicken on a serving platter, and spoon the sauce from the pan over the chicken. Makes 4–6 servings.

ZUCCHINI LASAGNA

1/2 cup	**panko breadcrumbs**
2 tablespoons	**butter or olive oil**
4–6	**firm zucchini,** cut lengthwise into 1/4-inch thick slices (you will need 24 slices)
	salt, to taste
1 package (10 ounces)	**frozen spinach,** thawed, thoroughly drained, and squeezed dry
2 cups	**marinara sauce,** divided
3/4 cup	**grated part-skim mozzarella cheese**
1 1/2 cups	**ricotta cheese**
1/2 cup plus more	**finely grated Parmesan cheese**
1	**egg,** lightly beaten
2–3 cloves	**garlic,** minced
1/2 teaspoon	**Italian seasoning blend**
	pepper, to taste
2 tablespoons	**thinly sliced fresh basil**

Preheat oven to 350 degrees. Prepare a 12-cup Bundt pan with nonstick cooking spray. In a small bowl, mix breadcrumbs and butter together. Dust the inside of the pan with the mixture.

Lay zucchini slices flat on a baking sheet, sprinkle with salt, and set aside for 15 minutes. In a medium bowl, combine spinach, 1/2 cup marinara sauce, cheeses, egg, garlic, Italian seasoning, salt, and pepper; mix until combined.

Wipe the zucchini slices with paper towels to remove excess liquid. Line the inside of the pan with the slices, placing the middle of the slice on the bottom of the pan and the ends going up the sides of the pan. Carefully spread the cheese mixture on the zucchini, and then bring the two ends of the zucchini slices together to form a roll. Pour 1/2 cup marinara sauce over the zucchini. Reserve the remaining marinara to serve on the side.

Bake for 25–30 minutes. Allow to rest for 10 minutes before carefully inverting onto a serving platter. Garnish with basil and Parmesan. Makes 6–8 servings.

CAKES

BROWNIE CHOCOLATE CAKE

1 box (12.75 ounces)	**chocolate cake mix**
1 box (18.5 ounces)	**fudge brownie mix**
4	**eggs**
1 1/4 cups	**water**
1 cup	**vegetable oil**

Chocolate Ganache

1/3 cup	**heavy cream**
1/2 cup	**chocolate chips**
	pinch of fleur de sel

Preheat oven to 350 degrees. Prepare a 12-cup Bundt pan with nonstick baking spray.

In a large bowl, add the cake mix, brownie mix, eggs, water, and oil; mix together until thoroughly combined. Pour batter into the pan. Bake for 50–55 minutes, or until toothpick inserted into the center comes out clean.

Let cake cool in pan for 10–15 minutes, but no longer. Turn the cake out onto a cooling rack and cool completely before transferring to serving plate.

To make the ganache, place the cream in a small microwave-safe glass bowl or measuring cup. Heat in the microwave for 30–45 seconds, making sure it doesn't bubble over; pour over chocolate chips. Whisk together until smooth. Drizzle over cooled cake, finishing with a sprinkle of fleur de sel. Makes 10–12 servings.

CELEBRATION CAKE

1 1/2 cups	**flour**
1/2 teaspoon	**baking soda**
1/2 teaspoon	**salt**
1/2 cup	**unsalted butter,** room temperature
3/4 cup	**sugar**
1/4 cup	**buttermilk**
1/2 cup	**sour cream**
2	**eggs,** room temperature, beaten
1/2 teaspoon	**vanilla**
1/4 cup	**sprinkles,** plus extra
2 cups	**powdered sugar**
2 tablespoons	**milk**

Preheat oven to 325 degrees. Prepare a 6-cup Bundt pan with nonstick baking spray.

In a medium bowl, whisk together the flour, baking soda, and salt. Add the butter, sugar, buttermilk, sour cream, eggs, and vanilla. Whisk together until combined. Gently fold in the sprinkles.

Spread batter evenly in the pan. Bake for 30 minutes and then check for doneness; bake an additional 5–10 minutes if necessary. Cool in pan on wire rack for 10 minutes then invert onto a cake plate to cool completely.

In a medium bowl, combine the powdered sugar and milk. Whisk well to eliminate lumps. Pour glaze over the cooled cake and add sprinkles with wild abandon. Makes 10–12 servings.

NOTE: Recipe can be doubled for use in a 12-cup Bundt pan.

RED VELVET CAKE

1 1/2 cups	**flour**
1 cup	**unsweetened cocoa powder**
2 teaspoons	**baking powder**
1 teaspoon	**baking soda**
1/2 teaspoon	**salt**
10 ounces	**cooked beets,** pureed
1 cup	**vegetable oil**
1/2 cup	**milk**
2 teaspoons	**sour cream**
1 teaspoon	**balsamic vinegar**
2	**eggs,** room temperature
1 1/3 cups	**sugar**

Cream Cheese Frosting

4 ounces	**cream cheese,** softened
1 cup	**powdered sugar**
2 teaspoons	**milk**

Preheat the oven to 350 degrees. Prepare a 12-cup Bundt pan with nonstick baking spray.

In a medium bowl, whisk together the flour, cocoa powder, baking powder, baking soda, and salt. In a separate bowl, blend together the beets, oil, milk, sour cream, vinegar, eggs, and sugar until thoroughly combined. Add the dry ingredients to the beet mixture and stir until combined.

Pour batter into the pan. Bake for 40 minutes, or until a skewer inserted into the center of the cake comes out clean. Place on wire rack and cool for 10–15 minutes before removing cake from pan. Turn cake out onto wire rack and allow to cool completely before frosting.

To make the frosting, cream the cream cheese, powdered sugar, and milk together until smooth. Spread on the top of the cooled cake. Makes 10–12 servings.

ITALIAN CASSATA CAKE

I container (15 ounces)	**ricotta cheese**
1/4 cup	**powdered sugar**
2 tablespoons	**orange juice**
2/3 cup	**diced candied fruit**
1 1/4 cups	**miniature semisweet chocolate chips,** divided
I package (3 ounces)	**ladyfingers,** split in half lengthwise
3 tablespoons	**half-and-half**
1/4 teaspoon	**instant coffee granules**
4 tablespoons	**butter**

Line a 12-cup Bundt pan with aluminum foil, pressing for a tight fit.

In a medium bowl, combine ricotta, sugar, and orange juice; beat until smooth. Fold in fruit and 1/4 cup chocolate chips; set aside.

Line the bottom and all sides of the pan with half of the ladyfingers, cut side in. Spoon filling evenly over the ladyfingers; press down and smooth top. Cover with remaining ladyfingers, cut sides down. Cover tightly with foil and refrigerate 4 hours or overnight.

About 30 minutes before serving, make a ganache by combining remaining chocolate chips, half-and-half, and coffee granules in a small saucepan over low heat until chocolate is melted, stirring often. Remove from heat and cool slightly. Add the butter, I tablespoon at a time, beating after each addition until mixture is well-blended. Refrigerate about 15 minutes, or until cold. Beat the chilled mixture with a hand mixer until thick enough to spread.

Carefully invert the cake onto a serving platter and remove the foil. Spread the ganache over the top and the sides. Store in refrigerator. Makes 8–10 servings.

LEMON BLUEBERRY POUND CAKE

1/3 cup	**butter,** softened
4 ounces	**cream cheese,** softened
2 cups	**sugar**
3	**eggs,** room temperature
1	**egg white**
1 tablespoon	**grated lemon peel**
2 teaspoons	**vanilla**
2 cups	**blueberries**
3 cups	**flour,** divided
1 teaspoon	**baking powder**
1/2 teaspoon	**baking soda**
1/2 teaspoon	**salt**
1 container (6 ounces)	**lemon or plain yogurt**
1 1/2 cups	**powdered sugar**
1/4 cup	**fresh lemon juice**

Preheat oven to 350 degrees. Grease and flour a 12-cup fluted tube or Bundt pan.

In a large bowl, cream butter, cream cheese, and sugar together until blended. Add eggs 1 at a time, and egg white, beating well after each addition. Beat in lemon peel and vanilla.

In a small bowl, toss blueberries with 2 tablespoons flour to coat. In another bowl, mix remaining flour with baking powder, baking soda, and salt; add to creamed mixture alternating with yogurt, beating after each addition just until combined. Fold in blueberries.

Transfer batter to prepared pan. Bake for 55–60 minutes, or until a skewer inserted into the center comes out clean. Cool in pan 10 minutes before inverting onto a wire rack; cool for 15 minutes.

In a small bowl, mix together powdered sugar and lemon juice until smooth. Gradually brush onto warm cake, about 1/3 at a time, allowing glaze to soak into cake before adding more. Cool completely. Makes 10–12 servings.

HUMMINGBIRD BUNDT

1 1/2 cups	**chopped pecans**
3 cups	**flour**
2 cups	**sugar**
1 teaspoon	**baking soda**
1 teaspoon	**ground cinnamon**
1/2 teaspoon	**salt**
3	**eggs,** room temperature, beaten
1 3/4 cups	**mashed ripe bananas** (about 4)
1 can (8 ounces)	**crushed pineapple,** with juice
3/4 cup	**canola oil**
1 1/2 teaspoons	**vanilla**

Glaze

4 ounces	**cream cheese,** cubed and softened
2 cups	**sifted powdered sugar**
1 teaspoon	**vanilla**
1–2 tablespoons	**milk**

Preheat oven to 350 degrees. Prepare a 12-cup Bundt pan with nonstick baking spray. Spread pecans in a single layer in a shallow pan and bake for 8–10 minutes, or until toasted and fragrant, stirring halfway through.

Stir together flour, sugar, baking soda, cinnamon, and salt in a large bowl; stir in eggs, bananas, pineapple and juice, oil, and vanilla, just until dry ingredients are moistened. Sprinkle 1 cup pecans into the pan and spoon batter over pecans.

Bake for 1 hour, or until a skewer inserted into the center comes out clean. Cool cake in pan on a wire rack 15 minutes. Invert cake onto wire rack and cool completely, about 2 hours, before glazing.

To make the glaze, whisk together the cream cheese, powdered sugar, vanilla, and milk, 1 teaspoon at a time, until glaze is smooth and a pouring consistency. Immediately pour glaze over cooled cake and sprinkle with remaining pecans. Makes 10–12 servings.

SNICKERS-FILLED BUNDT

¹/₂ cup plus extra	**unsweetened cocoa powder**
6 (1.61 ounces each)	**Snickers bars,** divided
1 cup	**unsalted butter**
¹/₂ teaspoon	**salt**
2 teaspoons	**vanilla,** divided
2 cups plus 2 tablespoons	**flour,** divided
1¹/₂ cups	**sugar**
1¹/₂ teaspoons	**baking soda**
1 cup	**chocolate milk**
2	**eggs,** room temperature, lightly beaten
¹/₂ cup	**sour cream**
8 ounces	**cream cheese,** softened
²/₃ cup	**powdered sugar**
1	**egg yolk**
¹/₂ cup	**chopped peanuts**
¹/₂ cup	**caramel sauce**
1 cup	**semisweet chocolate chips**
²/₃ cup	**heavy whipping cream**

Preheat oven to 350 degrees. Prepare a 12-cup Bundt pan with nonstick baking spray and dust with cocoa powder. Chop 3 candy bars; set aside.

Melt butter in a small saucepan over medium heat. Add cocoa and salt, whisking until smooth. Remove from heat and stir in 1 teaspoon vanilla; cool 5–10 minutes.

In a large bowl, stir together 2 cups flour, sugar, and baking soda. Slowly beat in butter mixture until moist crumbs form. Gradually add chocolate milk and eggs, beating well after each addition. Stir in sour cream; set aside.

Beat cream cheese in a separate bowl until smooth. Gradually beat in powdered sugar, egg yolk, remaining flour, and remaining vanilla. Stir in peanuts and caramel.

Pour about 4 cups of the chocolate batter into the pan. Spoon cream cheese mixture down the middle of batter, keeping away from the edges. Carefully place the chopped candy bars on top of the cream cheese mixture, and pour the remaining batter on top. Bake 45–55 minutes, or until a skewer inserted into the center comes out clean. Cool in pan on wire rack about 20 minutes. Invert cake onto wire rack and cool completely.

Place chocolate chips in a heatproof bowl. Heat the cream until hot, but not boiling and pour over chips; let sit for about 5 minutes, then whisk together until melted and smooth. Cool 10–20 minutes, or until slightly thickened. Pour over top of cake, allowing some to go down sides. Chop remaining candy bars and sprinkle over top of cake. Cover and store cake in refrigerator. Allow to come to room temperature before serving. Makes 10–12 servings.

CREAM CHEESE POUND CAKE

1 1/2 cups	**butter,** room temperature
8 ounces	**cream cheese,** room temperature
3 cups	**sugar**
6	**eggs,** room temperature
3 cups	**flour**
1 teaspoon	**salt**
1 tablespoon	**vanilla**

Preheat oven to 325 degrees. Prepare 12-cup Bundt or tube pan with nonstick baking spray.

In a large bowl, cream together the butter, cream cheese, and sugar until light and fluffy. Beat in eggs, 1 at a time. Add flour, salt, and vanilla; mix until just combined. Pour into prepared pan. Bake for 60–90 minutes, until golden brown and skewer inserted into the center of the cake comes out clean; check for doneness after 60 minutes. Makes 10 servings.

FUNFETTI CAKE

2 cups	**flour**
1 1/2 cups	**sugar**
4 teaspoons	**baking powder**
1/2 teaspoon	**salt**
2	**eggs,** room temperature
1 cup	**buttermilk,** room temperature
2/3 cup	**sour cream,** room temperature
1/2 cup	**vegetable oil**
2 teaspoons	**vanilla**
1/3 cup	**sprinkles**

Frosting

1/4 cup	**unsalted butter,** softened
2 cups	**powdered sugar**
2–3 teaspoons	**milk**
1/2 cup	**sprinkles**

Preheat oven to 350 degrees. Prepare a 12-cup Bundt pan with nonstick baking spray.

In a large bowl, add flour, sugar, baking powder, and salt; whisk to combine. In a medium bowl, add eggs, buttermilk, sour cream, oil, and vanilla; whisk to combine. Add the wet mixture to the dry, stirring lightly with a spoon or folding with a spatula until just combined. Small lumps will be present; don't overmix. Gently stir in the sprinkles.

Spoon the batter into the prepared pan and bake for 40–50 minutes (start checking after 40 minutes), or until center is set and a toothpick inserted in the center of the cake comes out clean. Cool in pan 10 minutes before inverting onto a wire rack; cool for 15 minutes.

To make the frosting, beat the butter, powdered sugar, and milk together until smooth. Stir in the sprinkles and spread over cooled cake. Makes 10–12 servings.

CITRUS OVERLOAD BUNDT CAKE

2	**lemons,** zested
1	**large orange,** zested
1	**blood orange,** zested
2³/₄ cups	**flour**
1¹/₂ cups	**sugar**
2 teaspoons	**baking powder**
1³/₄ teaspoons	**salt**
³/₄ cup	**sour cream,** room temperature
6	**eggs,** room temperature
³/₄ cup	**unsalted butter,** melted
¹/₃ cup	**fresh lemon juice** (from 1 to 2 lemons)
3 tablespoons	**fresh orange juice**
¹/₂ cup	**superfine sugar**
1 cup	**sifted powdered sugar**
2 to 3 tablespoons	**fresh blood orange juice**

Preheat oven to 350 degrees. Prepare a 12-cup Bundt pan with nonstick baking spray. Juice all citrus into a bowl, reserve remaining pulp from juicer and from peels, chop, and place into another bowl.

Sift together flour, sugar, baking powder, and salt into a bowl. Add sour cream; beat on medium speed until combined. Add eggs, 1 at a time, beating after each to combine. Beat in butter, citrus juice, and zest. Add pulp and beat just to combine. Transfer batter to pan. Bake for about 45 minutes, or until a toothpick inserted into the center comes out clean. Allow cake to cool in pan on a wire rack set over a baking sheet for 15 minutes. Invert cake onto rack and let cool for 10 more minutes.

In a saucepan, combine ¹/₃ cup lemon juice, 3 tablespoons orange juice, and superfine sugar; bring to a boil, stirring until sugar is dissolved. Boil 30 seconds more; set aside. In a bowl, whisk together the powdered sugar and blood orange juice to make a glaze.

Brush syrup over cake until all syrup is used. Allow to set for 5–10 minutes. Drizzle with glaze. Let cool completely. Makes 10–12 servings.

ZUCCOTTO BUNDT

1 (12 ounce)	**store-bought loaf pound cake**
1/4 cup	**brandy or apple juice**
6 ounces	**bittersweet chocolate,** chopped
1 teaspoon	**espresso**
1	**orange,** zested and juiced
2 cups	**chilled whipping cream,** divided
1/2 teaspoon	**almond extract**
1/4 cup	**powdered sugar**
1/2 cup	**sliced almonds,** toasted and coarsely crumbled
	unsweetened cocoa powder

Prepare a 12-cup Bundt pan with nonstick baking spray. Line the pan with plastic wrap.

Cut the pound cake crosswise into 1/3-inch-thick slices. Cut each slice diagonally in half into 2 triangles. Line the bottom and sides of the prepared pan with the cake triangles. Lightly brush half of the brandy over the cake to moisten. Reserve extra triangles.

In a large metal bowl set over a saucepan of simmering water, stir chocolate until melted; cool slightly. Stir in espresso, orange juice, and zest.

In a large bowl, beat 1 cup of cream until thick and fluffy. Fold one-fourth of whipped cream into the chocolate. Fold half of the remaining whipped cream into the chocolate mixture. Then fold in the remaining whipped cream. Spread the chocolate cream over the cake, covering completely and carving a 2-inch channel into the middle of the cake.

In another large bowl, add the remaining cream and almond extract. Beat on medium speed and gradually add the powdered sugar. Continue beating until firm peaks form. Fold in the almonds. Spoon the cream mixture into the channel.

Brush the remaining cake slices with brandy and arrange them over the cake, covering the filling completely and trimming to fit, if necessary. Cover the cake with plastic wrap and refrigerate at least 3 hours and up to 1 day. Remove the plastic wrap, invert the cake onto a platter, and then gently remove the pan and the remaining plastic wrap. Sift cocoa powder over top and serve. Makes 10–12 servings.

HARVEY WALLBANGER CAKE

1 box (15.25 ounces)	**yellow cake mix**
1 box (5.1 ounces)	**vanilla instant pudding**
$^1/_2$ cup	**vegetable oil**
4	**eggs,** room temperature
$^1/_4$ cup	**vodka or ginger ale**
$^1/_4$ cup	**Galliano, Triple Sec, or orange juice**
$^3/_4$ cup	**orange juice**

Preheat oven to 350 degrees. Prepare a 12-cup Bundt pan with nonstick baking spray.

In a large bowl, mix together cake mix, pudding mix, oil, eggs, vodka, Galliano, and orange juice; beat for 4 minutes. Pour batter into pan. Bake for 40–50 minutes, or until a skewer inserted into center of cake comes out clean. Allow to cool in the pan for 10 minutes before inverting onto wire rack to cool completely. Makes 12 servings.

FOURTH OF JULY BUNDT

1 1/2 cups	**flour**
1 1/2 teaspoons	**baking powder**
1/2 teaspoon	**salt**
3/4 cup plus 2 tablespoons	**unsalted butter,** softened
3/4 cup	**sugar**
1 can (12.5 ounces)	**almond cake and pastry filling**
2 teaspoons	**fresh lemon juice**
1 teaspoon	**almond extract**
1/2 teaspoon	**vanilla**
3	**eggs,** room temperature
1/4 teaspoon	**blue liquid food coloring**
1/8 teaspoon	**red liquid food coloring**
1 cup	**seedless raspberry or apricot jam**
	Chocolate Ganache (page 94)

Preheat oven to 350 degrees. Prepare a 12-cup Bundt pan with nonstick baking spray.

In a medium bowl, whisk flour, baking powder, and salt until evenly combined. In a large bowl, beat the butter and sugar on medium-high speed until pale and fluffy, about 3 minutes. Add almond filling, lemon juice, almond extract, and vanilla; beat until smooth. Add the eggs, 1 at a time, beating well after each addition. Add the flour mixture then stir with a rubber spatula until the batter is combined.

Divide the batter equally among 3 bowls. Stir blue food coloring in one bowl, red food coloring in the second bowl, and leave the third bowl of batter plain; set aside.

Warm the jam for 30 seconds in the microwave. Funnel the jam into a plastic decorating bottle.

Pour blue batter into the prepared pan and spread evenly. Pipe half of the jam mixture over top of the batter. Carefully pour plain batter over top of the jam. Pipe the remaining jam over top of the batter. Finish by carefully pouring red cake batter over top. Bake for 40 minutes and check for doneness, adding 5 additional minutes until a toothpick inserted into the center of the cake comes out clean.

Remove from oven and allow to cool for 10 minutes before carefully inverting onto a cake plate. Allow cake to cool for 15 minutes.

Pour Chocolate Ganache over the cooled cake. Allow to set. Makes 12 servings.

SOUR CREAM POUND CAKE

1 cup	**butter,** room temperature
3 cups	**sugar**
6	**eggs,** room temperature
$1/4$ teaspoon	**baking soda**
8 ounces	**sour cream,** room temperature
3 cups	**flour**
$1^1/2$ teaspoons	**vanilla**

Preheat oven to 350 degrees. Prepare a 12-cup Bundt pan with nonstick baking spray. Use the second rack from the bottom in your oven.

In a large bowl, cream butter and sugar together. Add eggs 1 at a time, beating well after each addition. Fold baking soda into sour cream. Add half the flour and half the sour cream to egg mixture; beat well. Add remaining flour, sour cream, and vanilla. Mix well and pour the batter into the pan. Bake for 1 hour and 15 minutes, or until a skewer inserted into the center comes out clean. Cool in pan for 10 minutes and invert onto wire rack to cool completely. Makes 10–12 servings.

MASCARPONE-OREO FILLED CHOCOLATE CAKE

1 3/4 cups	**flour**
3/4 cup	**unsweetened cocoa powder**
1 3/4 cups	**sugar**
2 teaspoons	**baking soda**
1 teaspoon	**baking powder**
1 teaspoon	**salt**
1/2 cup	**vegetable oil**
2	**eggs,** room temperature
3/4 cup	**sour cream,** room temperature
1/2 cup	**buttermilk,** room temperature
2 teaspoons	**vanilla**
1/2 cup	**boiling water**

Filling

12 ounces	**mascarpone cheese,** room temperature
1	**egg,** room temperature
1/4 cup	**sugar**
1/2 teaspoon	**vanilla**
1 cup	**Oreo cookies,** processed into crumbs
	chocolate ganache, optional
	whipped cream, optional

Preheat oven to 350 degrees. Prepare a 12-cup Bundt pan with nonstick baking spray.

In a large bowl, whisk together flour, cocoa, sugar, baking soda, baking powder, and salt; set aside. In another large bowl, mix the oil, eggs, sour cream, buttermilk, and vanilla together until combined. Pour wet ingredients into dry ingredients, add boiling water, and whisk until batter is combined; set aside.

For the filling, beat cheese on high speed until light and fluffy. Beat in egg, sugar, vanilla, and Oreos on medium-high speed until combined.

Pour half of the cake batter evenly into the prepared pan. Spread all of the cookie filling evenly over top but avoid touching the sides of the pan. (Using a small scoop helps here.) Pour the remaining batter evenly over top.

Bake for 45–55 minutes, until a toothpick inserted into the center of the cake comes out mostly clean with just a couple of lightly moist crumbs.

Remove from the oven and allow to cool for 1 hour in the pan (as this is a heavier cake, it needs time to set). Invert the cooled cake onto a wire rack or serving dish. Allow cake to cool completely then refrigerate for 2 hours. Garnish with optional toppings, such as chocolate ganache or whipped cream. Store in refrigerator. Makes 10–12 servings.

EASY ICE CREAM CAKE

1 package (16 ounce)	**pound cake mix**
28 ounces	**softened ice cream,** of choice

Prepare a 12-cup Bundt pan with nonstick baking spray.

Prepare and bake the pound cake according to package directions. Cool for 10 minutes before inverting cake onto a work surface. Allow to cool completely.

Slice cake in half lengthwise. Line the cooled pan with plastic wrap. Return top half of the cake to pan, spread with ice cream, and top with bottom half of the cake. Wrap the pan in plastic wrap and place in freezer for at least 2 hours. When ready to serve, use plastic wrap to remove cake from the pan and invert onto a serving platter. Serve immediately. Makes 8–10 servings.

APPLE DUMPLING CAKE

¹/₂ cup	**butter,** melted
3	**eggs,** slightly beaten, room temperature
¹/₂ cup	**sugar**
¹/₂ cup	**firmly packed brown sugar**
¹/₂ cup	**milk**
¹/₂ cup	**water**
¹/₂ cup	**plain Greek yogurt**
3 cups	**flour**
I teaspoon	**salt**
I tablespoon	**apple pie spice**
I teaspoon	**ground cinnamon,** plus more for dusting
I teaspoon	**baking soda**
3 cups	**diced apples**
I cup	**chopped pecans**
	ice cream, optional

Preheat oven to 350 degrees. Prepare a 12-cup Bundt pan with nonstick baking spray.

In a large bowl, mix the butter, eggs, and sugars until combined. In another bowl, mix the milk, water, and yogurt together; stir into the butter mixture. Sift together the flour, salt, apple pie spice, cinnamon, and baking soda; stir into the wet ingredients. Fold in the apples and pecans.

Pour the batter into the prepared pan and bake for I hour, or until a toothpick inserted into the center comes out clean. Allow to cool for 10 minutes then carefully invert onto a serving plate. Serve with cinnamon-dusted ice cream, if desired. Makes 10–12 servings.

STRAWBERRY SWIRL CREAM CHEESE POUND CAKE

1 1/2 cups	**butter,** room temperature
8 ounces	**cream cheese,** room temperature
3 cups	**sugar**
6	**eggs,** room temperature
3 cups	**flour**
1 teaspoon	**salt**
1 tablespoon	**vanilla**
1 cup	**good-quality strawberry jam,** room temperature

Preheat oven to 325 degrees. Prepare a 12-cup Bundt or tube pan with nonstick baking spray.

In a large bowl, cream together butter, cream cheese, and sugar until light and fluffy. Add eggs, 1 at a time, beating after each addition. Add flour, salt, and vanilla. Mix until just combined, but do not overmix. Pour into prepared pan. Drop spoonfuls of jam over the top, and with a skewer, swirl the jam throughout the batter.

Bake for 80–90 minutes, until golden brown and skewer inserted into the center of the cake comes out clean. Check after 1 hour for doneness. Cool in pan 10 minutes before inverting onto a wire rack; cool for 15 minutes. Makes 10–12 servings.

VARIATION: Substitute a different fruit jam for a swirl of your choice.

PUMPKIN POUND CAKE

2³/₄ cups	**sugar**
1¹/₂ cups	**butter,** softened
1 teaspoon	**vanilla**
6	**eggs,** room temperature
3 cups	**flour**
¹/₂ teaspoon	**baking powder**
¹/₂ teaspoon	**salt**
³/₄ teaspoon	**ground cinnamon**
¹/₂ teaspoon	**ground ginger**
¹/₄ teaspoon	**ground cloves**
1 cup	**pumpkin puree** (not pumpkin pie mix)

Preheat oven to 350 degrees. Prepare a 12-cup Bundt pan with nonstick baking spray.

In large bowl, beat sugar and butter until light and fluffy. Add vanilla. Add in eggs, 1 at a time, beating after each addition until blended. In small bowl, mix flour, baking powder, salt, cinnamon, ginger, and cloves. Alternate adding dry ingredients and pumpkin to butter mixture, beating well after each addition. Pour batter into prepared pan.

Bake for 60 minutes, or until a toothpick inserted into the center of the cake comes out clean. Cool for 15 minutes before inverting onto a serving plate. Cool completely. Makes 12 servings.

BERRY-FILLED BUNDT CAKE

2 1/2 cups plus 2 tablespoons **flour,** divided
2 teaspoons **baking powder**
1 teaspoon **salt**
1 cup plus 1 tablespoon **unsalted butter,** softened, divided
1 3/4 cups **sugar**
1 **lemon,** zested
3 **eggs**
1/2 teaspoon **vanilla**
3/4 cup **buttermilk,** room temperature
3 cups **mixed berries,** of choice
1 cup plus 2 tablespoons **powdered sugar**
4 tablespoons **fresh lemon juice**

Preheat oven to 350 degrees. Prepare a 10-cup Bundt pan with nonstick baking spray. In a medium bowl, mix 2 1/2 cups flour, baking powder, and salt and combine thoroughly.

In a separate large bowl, add 1 cup butter, sugar, and lemon zest and beat on high speed for about 5 minutes. Add eggs and vanilla and continue beating until well-incorporated. Turn mixer to low speed, and alternate adding flour mixture and buttermilk, mixing to incorporate between additions.

In a separate bowl, combine berries with 2 tablespoons flour. Using a spatula, carefully fold berries into cake batter. Pour batter gently into prepared pan.

Bake for 60 minutes or until a toothpick inserted into the center comes out clean. Remove the pan from oven and cool for 40 minutes on wire rack. Carefully invert the cake onto a cake plate.

To make a glaze, whisk powdered sugar, lemon juice, and remaining butter in a small bowl until very thick. Spread glaze over the top of the cooled cake. Makes 10–12 servings.

HOLIDAY FRUIT CAKE

8 ounces	**cream cheese,** softened
I cup	**butter,** softened
I¹/₂ cups	**sugar**
4	**eggs**
I¹/₂ teaspoons	**vanilla**
2¹/₄ cups	**cake flour,** divided
I¹/₂ teaspoons	**baking powder**
I cup	**chopped pecans**
I¹/₂ cups	**red and green candied cherries**

Glaze

I¹/₂ cups	**powdered sugar**
3–4 tablespoons	**milk**
¹/₂ teaspoon	**vanilla**
pinch of	**salt**
	additional candied cherries

Preheat oven to 325 degrees. Prepare a 10-cup Bundt pan with nonstick baking spray.

In a large bowl, beat cream cheese, butter, and sugar until fluffy. Add eggs, 1 at a time, beating well after each addition. Add vanilla. Combine 2 cups flour and baking powder; gradually beat into batter. Combine pecans, cherries, and remaining flour; fold into batter.

Pour batter into the prepared pan and bake for 60 minutes or until a toothpick inserted in the center comes out clean. Cool 10 minutes; remove from pan to a wire rack to cool completely.

To make the glaze, combine powdered sugar, milk, vanilla, and salt; drizzle over cake. Garnish with cherries. Makes 10–12 servings.

DESSERTS

ITALIAN FLAG BUNDT

1 1/2 cups	**flour**
1 1/2 teaspoons	**baking powder**
1/2 teaspoon	**salt**
3/4 cup plus 2 tablespoons	**unsalted butter,** softened
3/4 cup	**sugar**
1 can (12.5 ounces)	**almond cake and pastry filling**
2 teaspoons	**fresh lemon juice**
1 teaspoon	**almond extract**
1/2 teaspoon	**vanilla**
3	**eggs,** room temperature
1/8 teaspoon	**green liquid food coloring**
1/4 teaspoon	**red liquid food coloring**
1 cup	**seedless raspberry or apricot jam**
	Chocolate Ganache (page 94)

Preheat oven to 350 degrees. Prepare 12-cup Bundt or tube pan with nonstick baking spray.

In a medium bowl, whisk flour, baking powder, and salt until evenly combined. In a large bowl, beat butter and sugar on medium-high speed until pale and fluffy, about 3 minutes. Add almond filling, lemon juice, almond extract, and vanilla; beat until smooth. Add eggs, 1 at a time, beating well after each addition. Add the flour mixture then stir with a rubber spatula until the batter is combined.

Divide the batter equally among 3 bowls. Stir green food coloring in one bowl, red food coloring in the second bowl, and leave the third bowl plain; set aside.

Warm the jam for 30 seconds in the microwave. Funnel the jam into a plastic decorating bottle.

Pour the red batter into the prepared pan and spread evenly. Pipe half of the jam mixture on top of batter. Carefully pour the plain batter over top of the jam. Pipe the remaining jam over top of the batter. Finish by carefully pouring the green cake batter over top.

Bake for 40 minutes and check for doneness, adding 5 additional minutes until a toothpick inserted into the center of the cake comes out clean.

Remove from oven and cool for 10 minutes before carefully inverting onto a cake plate. Allow cake to cool for 15 minutes.

Pour Chocolate Ganache over the cooled cake. Allow to set. Makes 12 servings.

PEACH CRISP

2 cans (21 ounces each)	**peach pie filling**
2 cups	**biscuit mix**
$1/2$ cup	**sugar**
1 cup	**butter,** melted
$1/2$ cup	**chopped pecans**
	vanilla ice cream, optional

Preheat oven to 375 degrees. Prepare a 12-cup Bundt pan with nonstick cooking spray.

Pour peach filling into the bottom of the pan, sprinkle biscuit mix on top of peaches, and sprinkle sugar on top. Pour butter over sugar, making sure to coat everything entirely. Scatter pecans on top. Bake for 45 minutes until lightly browned and bubbly. Remove from oven and scoop into serving bowls. Serve with vanilla ice cream if desired. Makes 12 servings.

CHOCOLATE MARSHMALLOW RICE CRISP RING

4 ounces	**semisweet chocolate chips**
2 tablespoons	**butter**
I bag (10.5 ounces)	**mini marshmallows**
6 cups	**chocolate rice crisp cereal**
I cup	**salted dry roasted peanuts**
I cup	**candy-coated chocolate pieces**

Spray a 12-cup Bundt pan with nonstick cooking spray.

Place the chocolate and butter in a large microwave-safe bowl. Microwave on high for I minute, stirring once during heating. Remove from microwave and stir until melted and smooth. Stir in the marshmallows. Microwave on high for I minute, until melted and mixture is smooth.

Add the cereal and peanuts. Stir until coated and well-combined. Add the candy (these are added last so the mixture won't melt them). Transfer mixture to prepared pan, pressing down with fingertips. Let stand for I hour; in warm weather, put in refrigerator to set.

Loosen with knife or metal spatula to unmold. Run a spatula all around the edges to pop out. Invert onto a plate and cut in slices to serve. Store in covered container at room temperature for up to 3 days. Makes 10–12 servings.

VARIATIONS: Instead of candy-coated chocolate pieces, add chopped candy bars.

APPLE CINNAMON DESSERT

3	**apples,** peeled, cored and cut into thin wedges
2 cups plus 5 tablespoons	**sugar,** divided
2 teaspoons	**ground cinnamon**
3 cups	**flour**
3 teaspoons	**baking powder**
4	**eggs**
I cup	**vegetable oil**
2 1/2 teaspoons	**vanilla**
2/3 cup	**fresh orange juice**

Preheat oven to 350 degrees. Prepare a 10-cup Bundt pan with nonstick cooking spray.

In a medium bowl, combine the apples, 5 tablespoons sugar, and cinnamon; set aside.

Sift together flour and baking powder; set aside. In a large bowl, mix together eggs and remaining sugar. Stir in oil, vanilla, and orange juice, mixing until blended. Make a well in the center of dry ingredients and pour in orange juice mixture. Stir just until combined.

Layer batter and apple mixture in the prepared pan, beginning and ending with the batter. Bake for 70 minutes, or until a toothpick inserted into the center of the cake comes out clean. Allow to cool before inverting onto a cake plate. Makes 12 servings.

JENNY'S ICE CREAM CAKE

¹/₂ gallon	**chocolate ice cream,** softened
I small jar	**good-quality caramel sauce**
I package (9 ounces)	**thin chocolate wafer cookies**

Line a 12-cup Bundt pan with plastic wrap.

Carefully scoop one-third of the ice cream into the bottom of the pan. Drizzle one-half of the caramel sauce on top of the ice cream. Arrange a single layer of cookies on top of ice cream. Repeat with another layer of ice cream, caramel, and cookies. Use the remaining ice cream for the last layer. Cover with plastic wrap. Press down gently. Freeze for at least 2 hours. Remove top plastic wrap, invert onto a platter, and remove bottom plastic wrap. Makes 8–10 servings.

PEACH COBBLER

2 1/4 cups	**biscuit mix,** divided
1/2 cup plus 2 tablespoons	**sugar,** divided
1 cup plus 3 tablespoons	**butter,** melted, divided
2 cans (21 ounces each)	**peach pie filling**
	vanilla ice cream, optional

Preheat oven to 375 degrees. Prepare a 12-cup Bundt pan with nonstick baking spray with flour.

In a medium bowl, mix 1/4 cup biscuit mix, 2 tablespoons sugar, and 3 tablespoons butter. Line the bottom of prepared pan with this mixture. Pour the peach pie filling over top. Sprinkle remaining biscuit mix over top of the peaches. Then sprinkle remaining sugar over top of the biscuit mix. Pour remaining butter over all, making sure to coat everything entirely.

Bake for 45 minutes. Allow to cool for 10 minutes then carefully invert onto a serving platter. Serve with vanilla ice cream, if desired. Makes 8–10 servings.

STRAWBERRY GELATIN MOLD

3 boxes (6 ounces each) **strawberry gelatin**
5 cups **boiling water,** divided
3 cups **cold water,** divided
ice water in a large bowl
I cup **sliced strawberries,** plus extra
I can **sweetened condensed milk**
mint leaves, optional

Prepare a 10-cup Bundt pan with nonstick cooking spray.

In a large bowl, dissolve 2 packages gelatin into 4 cups boiling water. Add 2 cups cold water to the bowl. Set the bowl with the gelatin into a larger bowl filled with ice water. Stir the gelatin occasionally for 30 minutes until it becomes a gel-like consistency.

Stir in the strawberries and pour into the prepared pan. Place in the refrigerator and chill for 15–20 minutes.

While the gelatin is chilling, dissolve the third package of gelatin into I cup boiling water. Add the remaining cold water once the gelatin powder has been dissolved. Stir in the condensed milk and let the mixture come to room temperature, about 15 minutes.

Check the gelatin in the refrigerator; it should be firm to the touch. Carefully pour the creamy gelatin onto the fruit gelatin in the pan. Let the gelatin set in the refrigerator overnight.

When removing from the mold, place a large plate on top of the pan and flip in one swift movement. If the gelatin seems to be having a hard time coming out of the mold, heat the pan slightly by dipping the bottom of the pan in warm water for I minute.

Decorate with mint leaves and cut strawberries, if desired. Makes 10–12 servings.

FRUIT TERRINE

4 cups	**apple juice,** divided
4 packets	**unflavored gelatin**
3 tablespoons	**sugar**
I tablespoon	**freshly squeezed lemon juice**
12 ounces	**fresh raspberries**
2	**fresh mangoes,** peeled and cut into ¹/₂-inch pieces
I pound	**fresh strawberries,** cut into ¹/₂-inch pieces
I pound	**green grapes,** halved
I pound	**red grapes,** halved, plus more for garnish
	mint leaves, optional

Lightly prepare a 12-cup Bundt pan with nonstick cooking spray and, using a paper towel, wipe the spray evenly through the interior of the pan.

Pour I cup apple juice into a large bowl and sprinkle with all gelatin packets; set aside.

In a small saucepan, bring to boil remaining apple juice, sugar, and lemon juice. Pour into bowl with apple juice mixture and whisk well to dissolve gelatin. Set aside to cool.

Place fruit into pan in the following order, raspberries, mangoes, strawberries, green grapes, and red grapes, spreading each fruit equally in pan. Add a few mint leaves in between each layer if desired. Carefully pour gelatin mixture over fruit in the pan, pushing down grapes to make sure they are covered. Refrigerate for at least 4 hours for gelatin to set.

To unmold the terrine, place the bottom of the pan in a larger pan of warm water for about I minute. Cover the dessert with a serving platter and quickly turn it over. Place additional red grapes around the dessert with mint sprigs if desired. Makes 12–14 servings.

BANANA PUDDING DESSERT

1 cup	**unsalted butter,** softened
2 cups	**sugar**
5	**eggs**
1 cup	**whole milk**
1 teaspoon	**vanilla**
3 cups	**flour**
1 box (3.4 ounces)	**banana cream instant pudding mix**
1/2 teaspoon	**baking powder**
1/4 teaspoon	**salt**
2	**bananas,** mashed
2	**bananas,** thinly sliced

Icing

1 1/2 cups	**powdered sugar**
2 tablespoons	**whole milk**

Preheat oven to 350 degrees. Prepare a 12-cup Bundt pan with nonstick cooking spray.

In the bowl of a stand mixer, beat butter and sugar until combined. Add the eggs,1 at a time, and beat until incorporated. With the mixer on low speed, slowly beat in milk and vanilla until smooth.

In a separate bowl, whisk together flour, pudding mix, baking powder and salt. Add to wet ingredients, 1 cup at a time, until just combined. Stir in mashed and sliced bananas until evenly distributed.

Spread mixture evenly into prepared pan. Bake for 60 minutes or until a toothpick inserted in the center comes out clean. Let cool in pan 10 minutes before inverting onto a wire rack to cool completely.

For the icing, whisk together powdered sugar and milk until smooth and of drizzling consistency. Add more powdered sugar if too thin or more milk if too thick.

Transfer cake to a cake stand or serving platter and drizzle with icing. Makes 12 servings.

CHERRY-ALMOND GELATIN MOLD

3 cups	**cold water,** divided
I teaspoon	**almond extract**
3 tablespoons	**unflavored gelatin powder**
8 ounces	**cream cheese**
I teaspoon	**vanilla**
I can (14 ounces)	**sweetened condensed milk**
I can (12 ounces)	**evaporated milk**
I box (6 ounces)	**cherry gelatin**
2 cups	**boiling water**
	sugared cherries
	sliced almonds

Prepare a 12-cup Bundt pan with nonstick cooking spray, place a layer of plastic wrap in the pan, and spray again.

In a small bowl, combine I cup cold water with almond extract, and then sprinkle the unflavored gelatin on top and let stand for about 10 minutes until it solidifies. Heat in the microwave until it turns liquid again, almost 40 seconds.

In a large bowl, beat cream cheese, gelatin mixture, vanilla, and both milks together on medium speed until combined. Carefully pour the cream cheese mixture into the pan and refrigerate for 2 hours.

In another large bowl, stir the cherry gelatin into the boiling water to dissolve and then add remaining cold water; mix well. Let cool to room temperature.

After the gelatin has cooled, take the pan from the refrigerator and remove the cream cheese mixture using the plastic wrap. Discard the plastic wrap and return the cream cheese layer to the pan. Pour the gelatin mixture over the cream cheese layer. It will float in the gelatin. Refrigerate again for another 2 hours or overnight to set completely.

When ready to serve, carefully flip mold onto serving platter and garnish with cherries and almonds. Makes 12–14 servings.

NOTES

METRIC CONVERSION CHART

Volume Measurements

U.S.	Metric
I teaspoon	5 ml
I tablespoon	I5 ml
$^1/_4$ cup	60 ml
$^1/_3$ cup	75 ml
$^1/_2$ cup	I25 ml
$^2/_3$ cup	I50 ml
$^3/_4$ cup	I75 ml
I cup	250 ml

Weight Measurements

U.S.	Metric
$^1/_2$ ounce	I5 g
I ounce	30 g
3 ounces	90 g
4 ounces	II5 g
8 ounces	225 g
I2 ounces	350 g
I pound	450 g
$2^1/_4$ pounds	I kg

Temperature Conversion

Fahrenheit	Celsius
250	I20
300	I50
325	I60
350	I80
375	I90
400	200
425	220
450	230

Yum! Check out these "101" favorites
for more tasty recipes:

Bacon	**More Bacon**
Beans	**More Ramen**
Beer	**More Slow Cooker**
Cake Mix	**Pumpkin**
Canned Biscuits	**Ramen Noodles**
Casserole	**Rice**
Chile Peppers	**Sheet Pan**
Dutch Oven	**Slow Cooker**
Grits	**Toaster Oven**
Instant Pot®	**Tortilla**
Jar	**Tots**

Each 128 pages, $9.99

Available at bookstores or directly from GIBBS SMITH
1.800.835.4993
www.gibbs-smith.com

ABOUT THE AUTHOR

Jenny Hartin is the founder of The Cookbook Junkies, a Facebook group that brings cookbook fanatics together, as well as a website of the same name. She is also the Director of Publicity for Eat Your Books and is well-known in the cookbook arena. Jenny spends a great deal of her time developing her own recipes, writing, cooking, and baking. This is her first cookbook. She lives in Colorado.